2ND EDITION

TALK READ TALK TALK WRITE

A practical routine for learning in all content areas (K-12)

NANCY MOTLEY

Published by Seidlitz Education
P.O. Box 166827
Irving, TX 75016
www.seidlitzeducation.com

For related titles and support materials visit www.seidlitzeducation.com.

8.17

What educators have to say about TRTW

TRTW is a practical process for teaching reading in content areas. The strategies are "tried and true," and our teachers immediately connect with Nancy because of the "real-life" teaching experiences she shares. Our teachers have found the TRTW strategies to be easy to implement and very usable. TRTW is not just good practice for ELL students; it is good practice for all students.

Carla Voelkel, Deputy Superintendent for Educational Services, Dickinson ISD

TRTW has enabled my students to truly enjoy reading by giving them a purpose to their reading. At each step of the TRTW process students are actively engaged, and they find relevance and importance to the content they are reading.

Edleen Aguilera-Nwachuku, 7th Grade Science/GT Teacher,
Garcia-Enriquez Middle School, San Elizario CISD

TRTW is one of the most practical guides to prepare ELL students to utilize academic language that I have read. The ideas resonate with teachers. When I walk into classrooms, I see the strategies permeating teacher and student work. So great to have an effective, systematic approach that is loved and implemented by teachers!

Karen Hickman, Deputy Superintendent of
Academic Achievement, Pasadena ISD

When using the TRTW teaching strategy with at-risk kids, the levels of participation and engagement greatly increase. The classroom environment becomes a safe place for effective writing and reading comprehension.

Katie Monaghan, High School English Teacher, Dickinson ISD

Our teachers have enthusiastically embraced the TRTW approach as a method for supporting all of our students, especially our Long-Term English Learners. They are able to easily integrate this strategy into their lessons because it is flexible, highly engaging, and complements our district curriculum and learning initiatives beautifully!

Danielle Emery, M.Ed., Secondary ESL Coordinator,
Learning & Teaching, Lewisville ISD

TABLE OF CONTENTS

AUTHOR'S NOTE

The response to Talk, Read, Talk, Write

has been very exciting and humbling. I have had the great honor to train and collaborate with thousands of teachers who are using TRTW as a platform for growing highly literate and articulate students. This 2nd edition was born out of this work. The most notable additions include:

Questions from the field

As teachers read the book, attend the training, and implement the TRTW approach, questions arise. In this brand new chapter, I provide the most common questions along with their respective answers.

Sample Lessons

The first edition offered four sample lessons. In this edition, there are 27 covering all grades and content areas, even foreign language and AVID!

Elementary application

Unlike the first edition that was solely focused on 6th-12th, the second edition addresses how TRTW looks in all grades K-12.

Format

The format of each chapter in this edition is "question and answer." In addition to a new planning template, there is also an index at the back of the book containing a list of every question addressed so that teachers have a quick reference. It is my hope that this question index makes this resource more accessible for those of us with limited time.

ACKNOWLEDGEMENTS

I'd like to begin with my heart: Marshall, Audrey, and Caroline. I could never do the work I love, which requires me to be away from home often, without your unconditional love and support. I'd also like to thank the entire Seidlitz Education team (Kathy, Michelle, Mónica, Michelle Y., Melinda B., Melinda M., Carol, Lora Beth, Tina, and of course, John) for inspiring, challenging, and encouraging me. Anne-Charlotte and Jenny, your dedicated efforts have made this book visually and linguistically beautiful. Finally, I'd like to end with my passion: teachers! Thank you for the extraordinary and really hard work you do every day. Especially thank you to all who collaborated with me on this book.

Nancy Motley

INTRODUCTION

When teachers think about asking students to talk, read, or write independently, they have many concerns. Mostly, they believe that students will find it difficult to complete these tasks on their own. Their apprehension is understandable. When students talk, they get off task; when students read, they might not comprehend the text; and when students write, they often produce low-quality responses. In a nutshell, students are not always successful when they work independently. How do we overcome these obstacles? While many teachers have used a trial and error approach to find a solution, this can waste valuable time. The instructional routine offered in *Talk, Read, Talk, Write* (TRTW), confirms that students can handle all of these components on their own. And, they can do it quite well. TRTW is a practical, literacy-based approach that develops a high level of independent speaking, reading, and writing skills for students, and it is applicable to all grade levels and content areas.

Looking back on my experiences as a teacher, I was always looking for ways to help my struggling students. I tried to plan and provide support so they could be successful. I did the best job I could, but I ran into a problem. I did not plan for providing support that leads to independence. I am a prime example of how teachers can create dependent students.

At the start of my career, I was teaching in a large urban school district with the majority of students reading below grade level. In addition, their oral and written communication skills were mostly underdeveloped. My students struggled with the majority of academic tasks. Intuitively, I knew that I needed to provide extra supports, or scaffolds, in order to ensure their success, and to do this, I had to visualize it happening. I pictured a staircase with the grade level standard at the top and my students standing at the bottom. I would hold their hands at the bottom of the stairs, teaching the content at their level, and then together we would walk up the stairs toward mastery of grade level concepts.

The problem with this image is that we never made it all the way up the stairs. In fact, we rarely made it past the first few steps. I was so focused on supporting and hand-holding that I trained my struggling students to need me too much. They didn't look up to climb the next stair on the staircase; they looked to the side, to reach for my hand and my help.

I became frustrated by my students' consistent minimal progress. I wanted to be the teacher who created astounding gains for her students, not the one whose students hovered near the bottom of the campus data charts. I was also exhausted. Planning support for each lesson was taxing, not to mention time consuming.

After several years of adjustments, my teaching practice and the way I visualized my role as teacher changed. I stopped asking myself, "What can I do to help my students?" I started asking, "How can I get my students to do this on their own?" I stopped holding their hands, and I started shortening the rope. Now, I pictured myself standing at the top of a mountain, the place where the grade level standard was situated. I saw some of my students standing at various places alongside the mountain, but many were at the base. I taught from the grade level standard, and I had a really long rope that I could throw, as far down as necessary, so that my struggling students could grab hold. Their job was to climb up the mountain, and my job was to help them…by shortening the rope.

My students still needed support, and I was still providing it, but my goal was to have them talk, read, and write without my help. However, in every student/teacher interaction, I knew I needed to inch them toward independence. Periodically, I would ask myself, "Can I shorten the rope now? Can they do a little more? How soon and how fast do I move them toward independence?"

I found that using the Talk, Read, Talk, Write routine in my classroom accelerated that shift toward independence. This approach moved my students, not in inches, but by leaps and bounds toward becoming independent readers, writers, and thinkers.

CHAPTER ONE

What is Talk, Read, Talk, Write?

The more that you read,
the more things you will know.
The more that you learn,
the more places you'll go.

–Dr. Seuss

As a reader, I love nonfiction. I am an avid history reader, love a good au-
tobiography, and do my best to read the news daily. Paradoxically, loving nonfiction
and being a successful reader of nonfiction only added to my strife as a teacher. For
quite a while, I was unsuccessful when teaching my students to read informational
text because I just couldn't put my finger on the difficulties they were having.

I began to look at all the statistics. I found that high school students' reading perfor-
mance had shown no improvement since 1971, and only 38% of high school seniors
scored at or above proficient, according to the National Assessment of Educational
Progress (Rampey et al., 2009). I also read that many teachers de-emphasize literacy practices central to comprehension because they feel the need to "teach to the
test." In actuality, their first and most basic responsibility is to address the linguistic
development of their students. If students cannot understand the text, they will not
pass the test. Therefore, in many cases, teachers of all grades and subjects have to
teach reading, writing, and speaking skills. This task is most often thought to be
the job of the elementary reading teacher, but if it is obvious that students cannot
comprehend what they are reading, they must be taught. I didn't have to look past
my own classroom to see that my students were struggling, and I knew I had to find
a way to reach them.

I didn't want to give up on teaching reading. I knew there had to be a way I could
help my students comprehend the textbooks and other informational material we
were reading in class. There had to be a way to erase those muddled looks from my
students' faces when we were in the middle of one of our reading tasks. The answer
to my problems came quite serendipitously one day.

This is the way it happened

1. WHAT ARE THE ORIGINS OF TRTW?

The TRTW framework was conceived after I received an email about my family's health insurance…of all things. The email stated that my company was offering employee health care, and they included an explanation of benefits with the email. I opened the attachments and began reading the documents. During my first attempt at reading the five pages of "Explanation of Benefits," the page of "Costs," and the three pages of "Enrollment Forms," I became overwhelmed by the technical jargon. Halfway through the second page, I realized that I couldn't remember what I just read. While my eyes had passed over each word, I had shut down. I was no longer comprehending the material, and I needed to find a different approach. I called my husband on the phone and asked, "Do you want to switch your health insurance plan to mine?"

He then began to ask me many questions that I couldn't answer…like, "What is the maximum payout, the Emergency Room deductible, the co-pay? What is included in the maternity coverage? Did the policy include vision and dental coverage, etc.?" We then had a long conversation about all the things I needed to look for in the attachments on the email. I hung up the phone, armed with my list. I had a purpose.

Now, I had to read through the insurance documents to find the answers to those questions. As I scoured all nine pages, my second attempt was much more fruitful than the first. I had a purpose for reading that propelled me through all the tedious, mind-numbing, and monotonous language of insurance policies. When I finished reading, I had either an answer for each question, or I had a question written down for the parts I couldn't yet understand.

I called my husband again. By this time, he had read the documents, and we discussed the answers to all of the questions. As we weighed the pros and cons of switching insurance companies, we kept looking back at the documents to support our thinking. The following day, we talked again and made our decision to switch companies. I responded to the original email, stating our intention to enroll, and I asked how to start the process.

I had an "Aha!" moment following this experience. This is exactly what my students experience when I assign a text for them to read! They go through the motions of reading, but inevitably their eyes glaze over, and there is little comprehension going on in their minds. Many of them are unable to remember, much less apply, what they have read later on in the lesson.

To find out what made my second attempt to find details more successful, I retraced my steps. First, I talked with my husband prior to reading. Together, we activated the knowledge that was critical to health insurance, and then we set a purpose for reading. The purpose was to answer some key questions. When I focused on answering those key questions, I was able to complete the reading. Next, I talked with my husband again to review the information I had learned.

Together, we analyzed the details and made an informed decision. Finally, I responded to the email inquiry.

My process to make meaning of the most dense, uninteresting text was: talk...then read...then talk some more...then write. Talk, Read, Talk, Write! Nothing had changed about the text. It was still dense and uninteresting, but everything about my process for engaging with the text had changed.

2. HOW DO YOU TEACH TRTW?

Talk, Read, Talk, Write (TRTW) is a classroom process that gives students an alternate and compelling way to access content area information, and every step of the process builds academic language. Think of TRTW as a replacement for the lecture approach. At its core, students read academic text. With a focus on the text rather than on the teacher "delivering" a lesson, students gain and deepen content understanding. Surrounding the core text are structured opportunities to talk and write about content.

The first step of TRTW, Talk #1, engages students in brief, structured conversations with each other and the teacher for the purpose of connecting to the topic, engaging the student, establishing prior knowledge, and setting a purpose for reading. In Chapter Two, I discuss ways to build this skill.

During the second step of TRTW, the Read section, students actively read an academic text. By active, I mean that they are doing some kind of writing to keep them on track, recall information, or ask questions about the content. There are many methods and graphic organizers that support active reading that I will discuss in Chapter Three.

During the third step, Talk #2, students dialogue with each other in order to process what they have read. Talk #2 also gives students a chance to prepare for upcoming writing activities. In Chapter Four, I examine this step in further detail.

The last step of TRTW is to Write. During this phase, students learn to express their thoughts about the content. Not only does this deepen student understanding, but it helps students become strong communicators, an important life skill. This step is described in Chapter Five. I present the TRTW process within the context of a 45-minute class period of science, math, social studies, and English language arts. My plans are based upon short texts of one to two pages. These plans can be shortened to the length of a word problem in math or expanded to include the complete text of a primary source document in social studies. The process is flexible, meaning that sometimes students may need to write before they talk, or partners may want to read together instead of independently. The non-negotiable part is that students, not teachers, do the actual talking, reading, and writing. When using this approach with students who are still learning to read, each step of this approach can also be a shared rather than independent task.

It is also important to note that the TRTW process is just one way to help students learn academic content. Incorporating the TRTW process in the classroom will not replace all other forms of lesson delivery. In fact, many teachers have incorporated the TRTW formatted lessons for 1-3 days per week with great success. This time allotment gives students significant and consistent opportunities to read, write, and talk about their learning. In addition, it allows plenty of time for teachers to use other instructional delivery models as well. The approaches to reading and writing outlined in the TRTW process are intended to help students process and demonstrate understanding of content area concepts. This process does not replace reading and writing for other purposes, such as literary analysis, free voluntary reading, or creative writing.

At the end of each chapter, the Campus Connections section includes discussion questions and practice tasks for teams of teachers. Campuses can use this section as a guide for a book study or as a resource for job-embedded professional development. My hope is to foster collaboration among teachers as they become skilled in implementing the TRTW process.

3. HOW DOES BELIEF AND RESPECT IN STUDENT ABILITY ENTER THE TRTW PROCESS?

Early in my career, I wanted to craft my lessons so that the students did all the "heavy lifting." While I knew this was a good idea, my students' cumulative folders and my personal experience told me otherwise. As I planned lessons, I constantly circled back to thinking, "There's no way Malcolm will be able to do this on his own," or, "My class will never stay on task if I give them this assignment," and even, "What about my 'invisible' students, the ones who are quietly struggling?" I had a conversation with my husband, however, that forever changed my thinking regarding my students' abilities to work independently, and it came at the hands of the children I know best, my own daughters.

One evening my husband, Marshall, and I were discussing our girls. At the time, they were ages 3 and 4. I was explaining how much trouble I was having getting them dressed and out the door each morning because they dawdle and argue with me.

Marshall said, "You get them dressed?"

"Of course I do, and I wish I could figure out how to make it go smoother."

He just grinned at me.

"What?!" I protested.

He said, "You know, Nancy, when you travel for work, and I am in charge in the morning, everything runs pretty smoothly."

At this point I was thinking, "Yeah, right!" but instead I said, "Oh really? Do tell."

"Well, it's like this," he began rather smugly. "Audrey and Caroline must get dressed first and once they come and show me they are dressed, I let them get their breakfast. Once they show me their breakfast is all gone, then they can do whatever they want until it is time to leave."

Incredulously, I asked, "And they do it?"

"I haven't dressed them in almost a year. Audrey makes cereal, and usually Caroline has a piece of toast or a cereal bar." I was speechless.

I made two very important connections after that conversation. Kids need adults who believe they can complete a task. They also need another set of expectations. They need to know that they will do what they are expected to do. Kids will follow the leader. Neither of my daughters ever said to me, "Daddy does it differently," or, "I have to dress myself when you're not here." My daughters deserved far more credit that I had given them. How does this knowledge translate to my classroom? It undeniably means that I need to believe and respect my students' abilities just as my husband believes and respects our daughters' abilities. Children can surprise their parents and their teachers when they are given independence.

4. WHAT ARE THE BENEFITS OF TRTW?

Currently, there are many middle and high school students who spend most class periods listening to lectures and taking notes. They move from one lecture, via PowerPoint, to the next, copying down key terms in their journals or filling in the blanks on pre-copied note pages. Sometimes, they have brief opportunities during a warm-up activity to apply knowledge learned the previous day, or they may have an opportunity at the end of class to talk to each other... if they finish all of their assigned work. But, consistently, they are missing the chance to self-assess and deepen their understanding of text.

Likewise, there are many elementary age students who spend much of their class time observing their teacher's mini lessons, watching as she records a few students' thinking on an anchor chart, and then copying the teacher's completed model of an assignment. The majority of students have very few chances to share their thinking during whole group instruction; most of their opportunities to read, write, and talk for authentic purposes are limited to the times when they are in small group instruction during reading class.

Teachers' instructional decisions and lesson delivery are directly related to the overwhelming amount of content for which they are responsible. They feel obligated to "cover it all" as they try to prepare students for standardized tests and keep on track with their pacing guide. Teachers feel significant pressure to teach too many concepts in too little time.

Because of the predominant focus on content, many classrooms have turned into places where teachers deliver and students receive information. At times, teachers feel relieved if they can get through the PowerPoint presentation (or mini-lesson) and have students fill in the notes (or complete an anchor chart) within the allotted class time. In a sense, they feel validated that they are delivering the content.

The goal of this TRTW resource is to shift our thinking about what teaching can look like. TRTW is designed to help us remove the heavy sigh of exhaustion at the end of the day. In its place, we end the day energized because the students did most of the thinking and talking. Then, instead of asking, "How can I possibly cover everything?" teachers can ask, "How can I be sure my students understand this?"

The focus of this book is not on writing. Instead, the focus is on the process that precedes writing. Students often think that a writing assignment means putting pen to paper immediately. TRTW guides students through a process that helps them think about and understand what they want to say.

The TRTW approach helps students make increased strides in the learning process. Students shift from listen and copy (with little retention of the information) to talk, read, talk, write (with significant retention of the information). After all, teaching content area reading gives students the skills they need to remember and the ability to reuse the information from their reading (Tovani, 2004).

5. WHAT KINDS OF BARRIERS STAND IN THE WAY OF THE TRTW PROCESS?

Educating students in today's standards-driven, high-stakes test environment is a difficult task, to be sure. Teachers are being asked to teach more material, in less time, to increasingly diverse groups of students. We have required initiatives encroaching on class time, and we are often frustrated by both the limited academic background knowledge that students possess and their apparent inability to remember previously taught concepts.

In our efforts to minimize these problems, we sometimes limit the amount of reading and writing students must do. Some teachers might say:

- *They can't read the textbook anyway, and even if they could, it would take the whole class time for them to finish it.*
- *By tomorrow they won't remember what they've read so I'll have to reteach it anyway.*
- *It would take my class most of the day to write a few sentences, and then I'll be three days behind on my pacing guide.*
- *It is so much easier to just break it down for them so they can understand it.*

Daniels and Zemelman (2004) explain it best when they write, "We chose our profession mainly because we love a subject–physics, mathematics, art, history, political science, biology, chemistry, literature, or foreign language."

In fact, it makes some of us wonder. We may even think, "I teach math, not language arts. It is not my job to teach reading and writing." This statement is often followed with, "As long as my students can do the math, I've done my job. As long as they can pass the test, I'm happy."

Teachers often focus on content to the exclusion of process. The state standards (TEKS and the Common Core State Standards - CCSS) address both content and process, but because teachers are more comfortable teaching content, they often never quite make it to process. The process is vital. When a process is used to teach content, students will be able to transfer skills more readily, and they will be able to retain content. TRTW is most certainly a transferable process, a routine that students can use everywhere.

6. WHY DO TEACHERS NEED TRTW?

Research says that approximately eight million young people between the fourth and twelfth grades struggle to read at grade level. It also tells us that 70% of older readers require some form of reading remediation. According to Reading Next: A Vision for Action and Research in Middle and High School Literacy, while this group of readers does not need help sounding out the words on a page, they do need help comprehending what they read. In addition, a full 70% of U.S. middle and high school students require differentiated instruction—that is, instruction targeted to their individual strengths and weaknesses (Biancarosa & Snow, 2006).

Reading Next also reveals that approximately 32% of high school graduates are not ready for college level English Composition courses (ACT, 2005), and approximately 40% of high school graduates lack the literacy skills employers seek (Achieve, Inc., 2005).

These are some staggering statistics, but wait, there are more! Every school day, almost seven thousand students drop out of high school (Biancarosa & Snow, 2006). The high school curriculum is so complex that students simply do not have the literacy skills to keep pace. Teachers, therefore, have to find a way to deliver content that is so literacy focused and directed that students will find success and not failure. And, they will stay in school.

On a positive note, a recent survey by the National Center for Literacy Education (NCLE) finds that, in the era of the Common Core State Standards, 77% of teachers are prioritizing literacy. This means that teachers of all disciplines will spend time collaborating on literacy plans that best serve students. "It's much more widely understood today that every educator has a responsibility to improve student literacy, which is the gateway to learning in all disciplines," said Kent Williamson, director of NCLE (Williamson, 2013).

7. WHAT DO EDUCATIONAL EXPERTS SAY IN SUPPORT OF TRTW?

Some influential educators and researchers have given some very sound reasons to use talking, reading, and writing skills as a basis for teaching.

- Students can develop deep conceptual knowledge in a discipline only by using the habits of reading, writing, talking, and thinking, valued and used in that discipline (McConachie et al., 2006).
- The classroom should become a reading community, a group of people who regularly read, talk, and write together (Daniels & Zemelman, 2004).
- Meaning does not arrive. It is constructed over time (Tovani, 2004).
- If we give students regular opportunities to read, write, and talk about academic concepts, the average student would be more intellectually attuned, informed, articulate, and ready to make his way into the world (Schmoker, 2011).

OVERVIEW OF THE TRTW APPROACH

Steps	Goal	Strategies
Talk #1	Engage with content concept and set a purpose for reading.	• Ask a Provocative Question • Make a Choice • Respond to a Visual • React to Quotation
Read	Read an academic text to develop content understanding.	• PAT List • Annotation • Highlighting PLUS
Talk #2	Process the text and prepare for writing.	• Envelope, Please! • Check-in Conversation
Write	Communicate content understanding.	• Clear Explanation • Make a Claim with Evidence

Each step of TRTW is vital to a student's ability to navigate content. Incorporating any one step will benefit students. Incorporating the process in its entirety, even sporadically, will benefit students. Embedding the process, in a compacted form, as a small part of lessons will benefit students. Embracing the entire process as part of regular instructional routine, however, will change students' educational careers. Most importantly, it will give them the gift of literacy for life.

CHAPTER TWO
Talk #1

Talk is social. Talk is context-embedded. Talk is engaging. Walk through any middle or high school corridor between classes or any elementary playground or lunchroom, and it is easy to see that talk is how kids of all ages engage in the world around them. To capitalize on this in a TRTW routine, a lesson can begin by using the very tool students use to navigate their world...TALK. Not only is it natural, but it taps prior knowledge that helps students make connections to the reading they will complete in class.

Conversation is the most powerful learning technology ever invented.

–Jay Cross

8. WHAT IS TALK #1?

Talk #1 is an open-ended conversation that is related to the lesson objectives; it engages and prepares students for reading. The conversation can be among students, or it can be between the teacher and the students. However, the Talk time should be balanced between the teacher and the students in order to accomplish the following goals:

• attract students' attention
• tap prior knowledge
• activate the line of thinking students will need to accomplish the reading task
• provide necessary pre-exposure to concepts addressed in the reading
• set the purpose for reading

As Schmoker (2011) states, students of all grade levels "will read with greater interest when we get their attention and when we give them a clear, legitimate task or purpose for their reading."

✔ Talk #1 is	✘ Talk #1 is NOT
brief (1-5 minutes).	long (anything more than 5 minutes).
structured so that all students get the opportunity to talk (ex: partners, table talk, etc.).	the teacher talking with 4-5 students who shout out and/or raise their hands to answer.
open-ended.	a search for one correct answer.
relevant, novel, and authentic.	an oral recap of yesterday's lesson.
non-threatening exposure to new terms/ideas.	asking students to find definitions for new terms/ideas.

9. HOW CAN STUDENTS BE HELD ACCOUNTABLE DURING THE TALK #1 SECTION?

Beginning a lesson with students talking to each other can create some serious stress for the teacher. The prospect of giving up control of the class often prompts many of the following thoughts: How will I ensure they are on task? What happens to the kids who won't talk? How will I ever get the students back on track? I know this class, and they'll just talk about whatever they want.

All of these concerns are legitimate worries that need to be addressed. In order for student talk to work, the conversation has to be explicitly structured and expectations have to be clear. Students have to be held accountable for meeting those expectations.

One method for structuring student conversations is called Q.S.S.S.A (Q Triple-S A) which stands for Question, Signal, Stem, Share, Assess (Seidlitz & Perryman, 2011). The following explanation details how it works:

Question

First, the teacher asks the class a question related to the concept. Asking open-ended questions—usually beginning with How or Why—helps ensure that student conversation is rich and significant.

Sounds like...

- *How is a presidential system different from a parliamentary system?*
- *What do you notice when you look at this picture?*
- *How can you determine if a chemical equation is balanced?*
- *Why is it important to use the order of operations?*
- *Do you agree with this statement?*
- *In this article, how does the author's word choice impact his message?*

10. Why TALK?

"When students talk, they think." (Frey & Fisher, 2011)

Some of the earliest educational theorists explain that social interaction and discourse are the primary means of learning (Piaget, 1928; Vygotsky, 1986). Therefore, giving students a brief, structured opportunity to talk about the concept of an upcoming task communicates the expectation for thinking, and it opens the door for content learning.

When a class begins with Talk, it creates a foundation for respect. In a respectful environment, students start off on an equal footing, and their confidence allows them to build background knowledge for the lesson at hand. The reason is simple. Students understand they are valued for who they are and what they think. This is the time—during Talk time—for teachers to access prior knowledge, ask thought-provoking questions, give opportunities for students to wrestle with new concepts, and allow students to interact with their peers. This is also the time for students to understand they are responsible for thinking, problem solving, and engaging with the lesson. In other words, this is the time to get students involved. The foundation of respect established during Talk time sets the stage for students to respond to difficult academic tasks. This confidence-building time helps students feel worthy of the challenge ahead.

Signal

Instead of calling on students who raise their hands or shout out, the teacher asks all students to give a signal when they are ready to answer the question. Asking for students to give a signal accomplishes two goals. First, it builds in "thinking time" for everyone. Second, it communicates a clear expectation for everyone to participate—by signaling—instead of just the few "high flyers" who normally contribute.

Sounds like...

- *When you're ready, give me a "thumbs up."*
- *Jot down your answer and then put your pen down.*
- *Think about the question. Show me a fist if you think you have an answer. Show an open palm if you are not sure of the answer.*
- *Put your hand on your head when you have an idea.*

Stem

The teacher gives students a stem or sentence starter to help them answer the question. The starter simply rephrases the question as a statement. The stem helps students use academic language in their responses. It also encourages students to communicate in complete sentences. Compare the two interactions below:

✘ Teacher A	✔ Teacher B
Teacher: What is the primary function of the respiratory system? Student A: Gets oxygen all through the body.	Teacher: What is the primary function of the respiratory system? Take a look at the stem on the board for your response. [The board reads: The primary function of the respiratory system is...] Student B: The primary function of the respiratory system is to get oxygen all through the body.

Both students knew the answer, but only Student B used the academic language of the lesson in a complete thought. The more often students respond using sentence stems and the more they hear other students using sentence stems, the more they internalize the academic terms. In addition, they learn the process of communicating in a more formal and academic manner. Stems can be posted in writing or given orally to students.

Sounds like...

- *A presidential system is different from a parliamentary because...*
- *In this picture I notice...*
- *I can determine if a chemical equation is balanced by...*
- *I agree/disagree because...*
- *It is important to use the order of operations because...*
- *In this article, the author's word-choice impacts his message by...*

Share

Now that students have thought about their responses and have a sentence stem to get them started, they are ready to talk. The teacher determines with whom they share their response. The most critical feature of sharing, however, is that ALL students participate. It is not realistic or effective to call on each student individually, so sharing takes the shape of students talking to each other. Everyone answers the question with his or her pre-assigned partner, triad, or group.

Sounds like...

- *Turn and tell your shoulder partner your answer.*
- *Share your responses at your table, beginning with the tallest person.*
- *Explain your thinking to your two lab partners.*

Additional supports:
- Students might share out with the whole class, with other students chorally repeating the speaker's response.
- Teacher may call on several students to generate possible responses so that partners can use those ideas or create their own.

Assess

After all students share with their partners or groups, the teacher randomly selects the student(s) to answer the question aloud for the entire class. The goal of this step is twofold: formative assessment and student accountability. When the teacher hears the responses of randomly selected students, she can accurately assess the class understanding of the concepts. If the responses are not on target, the teacher can adjust the lesson immediately to move it in the right direction. In addition to gaining an authentic check for understanding, randomly selecting students builds accountability. It ensures that students stay on task because they have to share with others. When students do not know when or if they will be called upon, they are inclined to actually do the thinking and talking as assigned. In other words, they will be prepared to respond during random selection.

It is important to let students know at the beginning of class that you will be using a system for random selection. We do not want to put students in a situation where they feel as though random selection is an "I gotcha." Before students share with their partner it is common to say,

Sounds like...

- *Using an app that allows the teacher to enter all students' names at the beginning of the year, the app chooses Ashley Smith. The teacher says: Ashley, you can share your your response...or one that you heard in your group. What was the impact of the 15th Amendment?*
- *If your birthday is in the summer, please stand up. You will be the one to explain your group response.*
- *Okay, who has the number 12 on his/her desk?*
- *Frank, please draw a name from the cup to see who will answer the question.*

"Remember, I'll be selecting some of you to share your thinking out loud to the class after you talk with your partner. This is your chance to prepare, and also get ideas from your partner if you are unsure or do not like your idea."

If a teacher asks questions using QSSSA, but does not assess through random selection, the process usually does not work. For example, if after students share with each other, the teacher calls on those who raise their hands, shout out, or volunteer, there is no incentive for other students to stay on task. Students determine quickly that the teacher won't require anything from them, so the sharing time becomes social time. If, however, the teacher randomly selects several students to respond after the sharing time, students will make the effort to have a response; it avoids embarrassment if called upon during the lesson. Random selection creates some positive peer pressure in the classroom.

11. WHAT STRATEGIES CAN I USE FOR TALK #1?

As long as all students get a chance to participate in the lesson, there are countless ways to begin a lesson with Talk. The talk should be directly related to the day's content, and it should be structured. In any case, it should be thought provoking. Once these guidelines are established, feel free to let creativity be the guide for the shape Talk #1 takes.

> *Top Four Strategies* for beginning a lesson with Talk:
> *1. Ask a Provocative/Interesting Question*
> *2. Make a Choice*
> *3. Respond to a Visual*
> *4. React to a Quotation*

1. Ask a Provocative/Interesting Question:

The teacher begins the lesson by asking the class a question. It cannot be just any question, however. It must be the type of question that calls, entices, or requires students to answer. Some words that come to mind when describing this kind of question are provocative, interesting, unusual, and relevant.

Sounds like...
- *What if...*
- *Do you think...? Why?*
- *Is it possible to...*
- *Do you agree with...?*

The following **EXAMPLES** and **NON-EXAMPLES** can help determine the way to engage in Talk #1. These examples/non-examples are presented to demonstrate how the TRTW approach looks/ sounds in the classroom. The non-examples are not necessarily samples of bad teaching; instead they allow the reader to identify the key features of the TRTW approach more clearly.

Non-example (Middle School Social Studies)

Teacher: Okay, class. Today we are going to finish reading Chapter 7, "Mesopotamia." Then you can use your notes to write a summary of what you have learned. Remember to pay close attention to the graph on page 332 because it will help you see the importance of the river systems. I think most of you have finished the section called "Early Foundations" so you only have five pages left, pages 331-335. Let's get started. Just raise your hand if you have any questions while you are reading. I'll stop class in about 15 minutes to go over exactly what I want you to include in the summaries.

 Example

In the Classroom: The graph on page 332 is displayed on the projector screen along with the following text: Imagine that you earn your living by raising goats. If you could pick any spot on this map to put your goat ranch, where would you put it? Why?

Teacher: Okay, class. Today we are going to finish reading Chapter 7, "Mesopotamia." Look up here so we can get started. I'm going to give you about one minute to make a decision. Be prepared to explain your decision to your partner. For your information, this same map is on page 332 in your book if you would like to take a closer look. *(The teacher waits for one minute.)* Okay, time's up. Everyone put your finger on the spot you feel will be the best place to raise your goats, and tell your partner why you selected that area. It should begin like this, "I selected this region because…" *(Students turn to share with each other. The teacher walks among the rows for 20-30 seconds to listen to student talk.)* Okay, partner #1 finish up so that partner #2 can talk. *(The teacher waits another 20-30 seconds.)* Okay, let's bring this to a conclusion. Everyone look up here. Raise your hand if you selected the same region as your partner. *(7 of 12 partnerships raise their hands.)* That is very interesting. Melanie, tell me the location you and your partner chose.

Melanie: The top right part. *(The teacher gestures for her to continue.)* We thought the mountains would be good for goats because we always see goats on mountainsides in our books.

Teacher: I think you are right. Goats are well suited to mountains. John, what do you and Pedro think? Tell me about the different regions you both chose.

Pedro: I picked the mountains.

Teacher: One minute, Pedro. Let's hear what John thinks. *(The teacher turns to make eye contact with John.)*

John: I picked the left side because of all the rivers. Goats need to drink water.

Frankie: That's right. My uncle has goats, and he lives in Corpus Christi. There are no mountains there, but there is a lot of water.

Teacher: Well I think you both make good points about the need for water. So now that everyone has begun to think about goat herds, let's look at our reading for today.

Non-example (Elementary English/Language Arts/Reading)

Teacher: Boys and girls, as soon as you put your backpacks away please come sit on the carpet. (All the students sit on the carpet.) Today we are going to talk about the parts of a book. *(Holding up* The Very Hungry Caterpillar.*)* All books have some things in common. Who can tell me one thing that makes this (pointing to the book) a book? Several hands shoot up.

Mariah (shouts out): The name of it!

Teacher: You're right, Mariah. All books have a name called the title. *(Adds this to the anchor chart titled: Part of a Book.)* Let's see who is sitting correctly. I like the way José is sitting. Yes, José what do you think?

José: The name on it tells who wrote it.

Teacher: You're right, José. Books have an author. That is the name of the person who wrote the book. Let's add "author" to our chart.

 *Example*

Teacher: Boys and girls, as soon as you put your backpacks away please come sit on the carpet. *(All the students sit on the carpet.)* Today I am going to ask you a very important question. When I ask it I want all of you to think about it. No shouting out, and no raising your hand. I just want you to think about your answer. *(Makes a gesture of putting her index finger on her forehead like she is thinking.)* My question is…How can you tell that this is a book? What are some things you see that all books have? *(Holding up* The Very Hungry Caterpillar.*)* Lets all think for awhile. *(Remains silent for 5-10 seconds.)*

Okay, if you have thought of one way you can tell that this is a book, show me by crossing your arms like this *(Models crossing arms across chest and many students begin to cross their arms.)* Once you think of one way you can tell that this is a book, show me. *(Repeats signal.)* Okay, it looks like everyone is ready with an idea. Instead of calling on some of you, I am going to let everyone share their idea with their elbow partner. Turn and face your elbow partner. *(This is pre-assigned.)* Before you share, listen to how I want you to talk. Tell your partner, "One way I can tell that this is a book is…" *(Stem is posted on the chart paper.)* Class repeats, "One way I can tell that this is a book is…" Okay, now turn and tell you partner, "One way I can tell that this is a book is…" Ready, go.

Elbow partners share their ideas with each other using the sentence stem for 20-30 seconds.

Teacher: Okay, finish up your sharing in 5, 4, 3, 2, 1. Great, turn and face me. *(Students shift back toward teacher.)* Now I'd like to hear some of your ideas. If I call on you, you can share your idea or you can share your partner's idea. Melissa, can you pick a name from our cup? (Melissa picks "Eric.")

Eric: It has a name.

Teacher: So one way…

Eric: One way I can tell that this is a book is because it has a name.

Teacher: Excellent. Books have titles. The title is the name of the book. Everyone repeat that with me: "The title is the name of the book." Great! Melissa, who's next?

 Non-example (Middle School Math):

In the Classroom: Students open their notebooks and begin to copy the problem on the board.

Teacher: Hi everyone. It's good to see you today. Let's begin today's warm up. It is exactly like your homework from last night so I'm only going to give you two minutes to compete the problem. When you finish, turn your paper over, and I will know when you are ready. Please make sure your homework is in the basket because I am going to check it. *(The teacher takes roll and checks homework for approximately 4 minutes.)*

Teacher: Okay, it looks like most of you have finished the problem so let's go over it together. Geraldine, what should I do first? *(Geraldine is silent so the teacher walks to her desk. She looks at her paper and finds that Geraldine has solved the problem correctly.)* You have the right answer. What did you do first?

Geraldine: Divide by 2.

Teacher: Excellent. What did you do next? *(Even though the teacher is speaking to Geraldine, Adonna answers.)*

Adonna: Convert to inches.

Teacher: Good! Now, remember what we do next… *(The teacher explains the rest of the problem.)*

 Example

In the Classroom: Students take out their journals. They look at the problem for the day. Written above the problem for the day is: Put your pencil down and think. What would be your third step if you were going to solve this problem right now?

Teacher: Hi everyone, it's good to see you today. Let's all focus on our warm up. Without actually solving the problem in your journal, think about your answer to this question. In about one minute, I'm going to ask you to tell your group what you think.

2. Make a Choice

This strategy involves presenting options to students and asking them to select one. It allows students to make a choice. They love to do this because it means they have some control. In a highly managed way, they get to decide something. Offering a choice to students communicates respect, and in turn, it increases engagement.

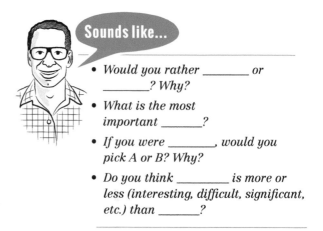

Sounds like...

- *Would you rather _____ or _____? Why?*
- *What is the most important _____?*
- *If you were _____, would you pick A or B? Why?*
- *Do you think _____ is more or less (interesting, difficult, significant, etc.) than _____?*

 X *Non-example (Elementary Social Studies)*

Teacher: Yesterday we watched a video about the basic needs of humans. We discussed the things that all of us need in order to live. What were our basic needs? *(Teacher accepts shout outs from students and calls on 1-2 students who raise their hand.)*

✔ *Example*

Teacher: Yesterday we talked about the basic needs we all have. Think about what we learned to answer this question: Would you rather have food to eat or a house to live in? If you had to pick just one, which one would you pick and why? *(Remains silent for 10 seconds. Gestures for those who raise their hands to put it down.)* Okay, if you would rather have food to eat go to the left side of the room *(gesture to the left)*, if you would rather have a home to live in, go to the right side of the room *(gesture to the right)*. *(Students move to each side of the room.)* Okay, make a bridge with a friend. *(Looks to make sure everyone has a partner.)* Talk with your partner to explain why you picked food *(pointing to the left)* and why you picked a home *(pointing to students on the right)*. Make sure that each partner gets a chance to tell his or her thinking.

 **Non-example** *(High School Science)*

Teacher: Okay, ladies and gentlemen, thanks for getting settled so quickly. We've spent the last few days discussing genetics. Who can tell me something they remember about traits? (*Many students raise their hands.*)

Teacher: Yes, Lizzie.

Lizzie: They can be dominant or recessive.

Teacher: Excellent. So what is the difference between a dominant and a recessive trait?

Lizzie: Well, you can always see the dominant trait, but um…the recessive one, you only see it when the dominant ones aren't there.

Teacher: Exactly right. Recessive alleles will only show in the absence of dominant alleles. That fact will be very important as you read today's article. Your purpose for reading is to explain…

 Example

Teacher: Good morning, ladies and gentlemen, thanks for getting settled so quickly. We have spent the last few days discussing genetics. Think about what you already know about traits. Do you think that recessive traits are more or less significant than dominant traits? I see some hands up already. For now, put your hands down and write the word "more" or "less" in your notebook. The question is: Are recessive traits more or less significant than dominant traits? (*The teacher checks to see that everyone has made a choice.*) Now, turn to your partner and explain why you thought recessive traits were more or less significant than dominant traits. (*Partnerships talk for about one minute, and then the teacher calls for their attention.*)

Teacher: Attention, everyone. If your last name begins with A through G, please stand up. We would like to hear what you think. (*Four students stand up, and each student explains an answer. Three students agree that recessive traits are less significant than dominant ones, while one student disagrees. After the last student shares, the teacher explains the purpose of today's lesson.*) I can tell that you were all thinking about the characteristics of both dominant and recessive alleles. Those characteristics, especially the fact that recessive alleles will only show in the absence of dominant alleles, will be very important as you read today's article. Your purpose for reading is to explain…

Non-example (English Language Arts)

Teacher: Good morning, everyone. We are about to wrap up our reading and discussion on Act 1 of *Romeo and Juliet*. Before we get started, let's look at where we stopped yesterday. My question is: Why did Romeo decide to go to the party? Think about that and jot down your answer on a sticky note. *(After a few seconds, some students begin to write. The teacher notices there are some ideas.)* Sondra, can you tell us why Romeo decided to go to the party?

Sondra: He only wanted to go because he thought Rosaline would be there.

Teacher: This is true. Thanks, Sondra. So we start our reading today with Romeo going to the party…

 Example

Teacher: Good morning, everyone. We are about to conclude our reading and discussion of Act 1 of *Romeo and Juliet*. Before we start, let's review the part we read yesterday. Remember, Romeo had just agreed to go to the party. My question is: Do you think that was a smart decision on Romeo's part? Think for a minute and then jot down your answer on a sticky note. *(After a few seconds, some students begin to write. After 20 seconds, all students in class begin to write.)* It looks like we have some opinions. Take a minute to share your notes with your partner. In one minute, we'll discuss your findings with the whole class. *(One minute passes, and the teacher chooses a person to share an answer. The teacher draws a stick with #17 on it from a cup.)* Who is #17?

Tran: I am.

Teacher: So Tran, what did you and your partner think about Romeo's decision? Do you think it was a smart choice?

Tran: We both said yes.

Teacher: Why?

Tran: If I really wanted to see a girl, I'd go to places where I thought she might be. Romeo thinks Rosaline will be there, so he makes a decision to go.

3. Respond to a Visual

Teachers can initiate conversation about a topic without using any words at all. Providing students with a thought-provoking or interesting picture, visual, or artifact related to the lesson's content goal is another good way to get students talking. Depending on the image, teachers may want to leave the response open ended, or they may provide a question about the picture to prompt students to respond in a certain way.

Sounds like...

- *Everyone take a minute to look at this picture and then you'll discuss it with your partner.*

- *What does this picture make you think about?*

- *What details stand out in this photo?*

- *Imagine you were in this picture…what would you hear, feel, smell, think, etc.?*

4. React to a Quotation

Posting a direct quote and asking students to react to it can spark great conversation. Quotations can come from many different sources. Using the words of someone that the students know personally, like a fellow teacher, the principal, or a community member usually creates instant engagement. Another approach is to quote famous people, especially those closely connected to students' worldviews, like pop culture icons. Depending on the content being taught, using direct quotations from historical figures or experts in the discipline is also an effective technique for bringing students into the lesson. A final approach for using quotations is to post the statement without sourcing it. Ask students to respond to it and then share who the source is. This works best when the words quoted are seemingly incongruous with the speaker who said them.

Sounds like...

- *Read Coach Mayberry's statement about hard work. Do you agree or disagree with his belief?*

- *Read the statement on the board, then talk with your partner about who you think said it.*

- *What is your reaction to this statement that President Roosevelt made? Do you think it still holds true today?*

Overview of TALK #1	Strategies
Ask a Provocative Question	• Post a thought-provoking question related to the content concept. • Give students an opportunity to discuss answers with each other.
Make a Choice	• Post a situation or question that requires students to make a choice. • Ask students to explain and defend choices with each other.
Respond to a Visual	• Post an interesting or dramatic visual related to the content concept. • Ask students to share their thoughts about the visual with each other.
React to a Quotation	• Post a quotation that is connected to the content concept. • Ask students to describe their (or their partner's) reaction/response to the quotation.

CAMPUS CONNECTIONS

Discuss

1. What reservations do we have about beginning class with student talk?

2. How can we tackle challenges that might arise during student talk?

3. How will Talk #1 impact our current warm-up, bell-ringer, or do now routines?

4. What resources do we have for finding interesting visuals?

Practice

1. Write 2-3 provocative questions for an upcoming unit.

2. Write and practice delivering 1-2 QSSSAs with your team (see p. 21-23 for examples).

CHAPTER THREE
Read

The Read section is the heart of the TRTW lesson. Reading, like any other skill, takes time and practice, and students need to read actively to engage with the text. When they read actively, they have a purpose for reading; they use prior knowledge and experiences to make sense of the text; they tap into new vocabulary and language presented in the book, and they find new reading strategies that work for them (Reichenberg, 2008). The goal of the Read section is to shift the balance from teaching to learning, from teacher-centered to student-centered, from the teacher providing information to the students reading information. Like any other skill, students must practice reading in order to improve.

Think before you speak.
Read before you think.
    –Fran Liebowitz

12. WHAT IS READ?

During the Read section of a TRTW lesson, the text, rather than the lecture or mini-lesson, is the manner in which students acquire new content area knowledge. Now, the student, not the teacher, can carry the workload.

Ideally, each individual student is reading a text to learn content. This is appropriate when students are able to decode and comprehend on their own. In the case of early elementary students, who are still learning to read, the Read section may look like a shared task with the teacher rather than an independent task.

In order to be successful, there are steps a reader has to take.
Since reading is not a passive activity, students have to "hold" their thinking by taking notes, highlighting, etc. These stored thoughts can then be accessed during the Talk #2 and the Write sections of TRTW.

✔ The READ section is	✘ The READ section is NOT
each student identifying text structure and reading with purpose.	the teacher reading the text aloud while students follow along.
each student reading individually **choral reading or partner reading is appropriate for beginning readers*	Round Robin reading, where students take turns reading sentences/sections aloud while other students follow along.
each student reading the entire selection.*	Jigsaw Reading, where each student reads only one section of the text and then explains it to others.

*The Read section for students with limited English proficiency or students who require reading accommodations may look somewhat different from this chart. (See pages 93-97 in Chapter 6, Special Populations)

The chart above is appropriate for a wide range of students, from those who possess basic decoding and comprehension skills all the way to those who possess highly refined literacy skills. (For students who are non-readers or emerging readers, see pages 105-106, "How can I implement TRTW in an Elementary Classroom?")

13. Why READ?

Literacy skills for the twenty-first century are far more complex than in previous generations (Goldman, 2012). In addition to the basics of reading comprehension, today's students must also know how to read with purpose, integrate new information, resolve conflicting content in different texts, and identify the writer's perspective (Biancarosa & Snow, 2006). Students can only learn these skills by reading. Because many students enter the classroom with underdeveloped literacy skills, we often replace reading tasks with lecture and interactive activities to ensure that students stay engaged and learn the content. Hoyt (1999) explains,

"...expository reading for many students is often a listening experience. Well-meaning teachers, concerned about textbooks that are too difficult, often create situations where one student reads from the text and others listen or attempt to follow along in the book. This situation does little to build conceptual understandings, and it can actually deter from the learning process as the listeners are engaging in very little reading."

When teachers "deliver" the curriculum to students, students lose the opportunity to construct meaning for themselves (Tovani, 2000). According to the Reading Next (2006) report (a meta-analysis of adolescent reading), three of the most statistically significant practices for increasing the academic achievement of middle and high school students included:

1. direct, explicit comprehension instruction
2. reading and writing skills embedded in content area classrooms
3. text-based collaborative learning

Put simply,

"When we routinely model and make explicit the methods adults use to read, think, and make connections, students learn to do it, too. Furthermore, they will see that such close, insightful reading is within their reach —that they can do such reading and thinking, which is central to an education." (Schmoker, 2011)

14. WHAT DO STUDENTS READ?

The content objectives—sometimes called student expectations, learning targets, lesson goals, or student outcomes—always drive the text selection. Many districts have protocols in place for how to plan, write, and communicate content objectives. While the format varies from school to school, all content objectives stem from state or national standards for each discipline.

When a teacher writes a content objective, TRTW provides a definitive pathway to meet the expectation. In a TRTW lesson, students are thinking, reading, talking, and writing for the purpose the teacher has set. It is important to note that the TRTW approach is not intended to replace content objectives, nor is it an add-on or enrichment activity. Instead, it gives teachers an avenue to meet content objectives head on.

For example, as a world geography teacher, my students need to learn the different forms of government that exist around the globe and how those governments impact the daily lives of citizens. Each step in the TRTW process is geared toward meeting that goal. Students talk, read, and write about the different forms of government and the impact it has on citizens.

15. WHERE CAN I FIND TEXTS?

The text itself is a vital part of a TRTW lesson. There are four main sources for text that most teachers use:

1. **Existing curriculum materials.** Many teachers already have usable text in the form of textbooks, district-created print resources, software licenses for online educational material, etc. This is a great starting point for finding text because these materials are already in our classrooms. We just have to take a little time to find out what they have to offer.

2. **Online resources.** There are innumerable sources for texts online. Below is a list of some popular sites for great text. Keep in mind each website's copyright statements as you determine how to use the material (i.e., ask students to read it online versus printing the article and making copies for students).
   - www.timeforkids.com – Weekly news magazine addressing a wide range of topics. K-6th.
   - www.teachingkidsnews.com – News articles posted daily. 2nd-8th.
   - www.dogonews.com – Current events articles connected to Common Core ELA, science, and social studies topics. Intended audience is K-12th.

- www.newsela.com – Articles addressing current events, science, kids, money, law, health, arts, sports. 6th-12th. There is also a *newsela* elementary version.
- www.kellygallagher.org – Author and teacher who posts an "Article of the Week" intended to build students' background knowledge. 9th-12th.
- www.tweentribune.com – Twice daily AP news articles, Lexile leveled for K-12th. Critical thinking questions and self-scoring quizzes also available. K-12th.
- www.naturalnews.com – News website about natural health and other science-related topics. In addition to articles, this website offers infographics, cartoons, and videos. 6th-12th.
- www.teenink.com – 100% of the content on the website is created and submitted by teens. Writing, art, photos, and forums for and by teens about topics they are connected to. 6th-12th.

3. **Student notes.** This option is often the most accessible form of text because students are reading their own work. Most students, especially secondary students, spend a great deal of time taking notes, either from their teachers' lessons or from reading material. Often the only other time they even look at those notes is just before test day. To increase their exposure to the content, teachers can use those notes as the reading material for follow-up lessons. In primary grades, a class-generated anchor chart can be thought of as "student notes."

4. **Teacher-created text.** The teacher writes the text for the lesson. Think of this as scripting the lecture or direct teach portion of the lesson. Rather than listening to you, students are reading. This may seem time consuming and daunting, but it is worth the effort. When teachers write the text themselves, they have the ability to eliminate some of the barriers that arise with other types of texts. The teacher has 100% control over the content that is communicated. He/she can ensure that what students are reading is tightly aligned to the standard, which is often not the case with online resources or out-of-date textbooks. Another benefit of writing the text is control over readability and word choice. The teacher can write with his/her students reading abilities in mind to make sure they will be able to comprehend it. A final reason to write the text yourself is to help create "buy in" for any reluctant or apathetic students. They are usually more willing to attempt the reading when I say, "Reading this won't be that bad. I wrote it myself, so it will sound just like me when you are reading."

16. HOW DO I TEACH READ?

We have to teach students to think of reading as a "tool for knowing" (Goldman, 2012). The opportunities students have to read should be directly aligned with a specific content concept. Rather than simply assigning page numbers, it is better to guide students in setting a clear purpose for reading as well as a process for making sense of the text.

For those who have never considered themselves a reading teacher, let's spend a little bit of time discussing what it means to make sense of text. Too often our students just run their eyes over the words until they find themselves at the end of the assignment. When asked a question about the reading, they respond with, "I don't know." Inevitably we take the class back to the text and spend time rereading and discussing those concepts we wanted them to figure out on their own. This leaves teachers thinking, "Why bother assigning the reading in the first place if I have to go back and reteach everything afterward?"

The solution to this predicament begins with explicitly defining "reading" for students. Reading is not figuring out how to pronounce all the words on the page. Reading is thinking. If students are not thinking about what they are reading, then they are not really reading. Telling students to think while they read isn't enough, either. Instead, many students need explicit instruction that shows what thinking looks and sounds like. There are two schools of thought about the way this should be taught in a content area classroom. They are: content area literacy and disciplinary literacy.

Content Area Literacy *focuses on*	Disciplinary Area Literacy *focuses on*
teaching students general reading strategies that help them make sense of any math, science, social studies, or language arts text.	teaching students content-specific strategies that help them read and think the way experts in that field of study read and think.

17. WHAT IS CONTENT AREA LITERACY?

Proponents of content area literacy explain that when we model and name the thought processes when reading with students, the abstract and internal skill of "making sense" of text becomes transparent, concrete, and most importantly, reproducible. Students will be able to replicate the same thought processes when they read. There is a deep and wide body of research related to these thought processes, also called thinking strategies, meta-cognition, reading strategies, or just plain, "things good readers do" (Harvey & Goudvis, 2000; Tovani, 2004; Gallagher, 2004).

The following brief overview of strategies is most helpful to students reading dense, content area material. These are the strategies good readers use when reading.

Asking Questions:

When readers encounter new information, questions usually arise. Struggling readers may view their questions as a sign of weakness, but stronger readers know their questions help them to stay focused. It happens very quietly in the background of a reader's mind during reading. Questions might take the shape of wonderings, confusion, or even challenges. The questions may be about the reader's relationship to the book, about the text itself, or about why the text is significant. They might look like this: What is the author trying to tell me? How is this text organized? What will I learn as I read? How is this book important in the overall scheme of things? Good readers know that questions help them stay engaged with the text. They also know that all types of questions are productive because they propel the reader to search for the answers.

Sounds like...

- *I wonder why...*
- *What does _____ mean?*
- *I am confused because...*
- *Why would the author...*
- *Why is _____ important?*

Making Connections/Prior Knowledge:

One of the most effective ways to remember new information is to link it with something already known. Making connections is about using a current inventory of prior knowledge and experiences to understand new information. Good readers make connections to their own experiences, to other concepts they've previously learned, and to the world around them. Linking the new information to ideas, feelings, and experiences increases readers' ability to retain and internalize new information.

Sounds like...

- *That reminds me of...*
- *This is similar to _____ because...*
- *When I read this, I thought of _____ because...*
- *Based on my prior experiences, I concluded...*

Sounds like...

- *The main point of this paragraph is...*
- *So the author is basically trying to say...*
- *One way to explain what I just read is...*

Summarizing/Paraphrasing:

Strong readers consistently process the new information they read into smaller, more manageable pieces. Throughout reading and when completing a text, readers summarize, or reduce the content into the most important ideas; they also paraphrase, or put the content into different words to make the meaning more clear. Conscientiously packaging new information into concise and simpler terms helps readers efficiently understand difficult text.

Determining Importance:

Reading expository or informational text is most challenging because it is packed with factual information. A single paragraph in a science textbook may have seven or eight new terms. Readers can easily become overwhelmed with all of the information–just like I was when I tried to read my insurance policy—if they do not know how to determine what is important and what can be left behind. Setting a clear purpose for reading is critical to determining importance. Having a purpose gives the reader a way to filter the information they encounter. Teaching students to use a filter as they read will help them stay focused and engaged with the text.

Sounds like...

- *I am reading to find out...*
- *I know _____ is important because...*
- *I need to remember...*
- *_____ is significant because...*

Sounds like...

- *I think _____ because the text says _____.*
- *I can infer that _____ because...*
- *The word _____ makes me think that...*

Making Inferences:

Making an inference involves using information from the text, along with personal knowledge, to decide something about a character or an event. When a reader makes an inference, he/she is making a claim that can be supported with evidence from the text. Making inferences is like reading between the lines. This reading strategy is both the most abstract and the most significant for students to master. Consistent modeling of how to make inferences is extremely important.

Visualizing:

Readers who consistently visualize while they read form pictures or movies in their minds; they literally see the information they are reading. These images help readers organize what they read, and it helps them visualize the text in a three-dimensional way. Readers may adapt the visuals as they read to form more precise pictures in their minds.

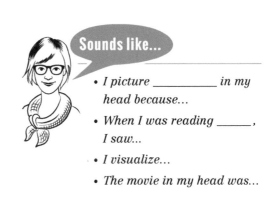

Sounds like...

- *I picture _____ in my head because...*
- *When I was reading _____, I saw...*
- *I visualize...*
- *The movie in my head was...*

18. WHAT IS DISCIPLINARY LITERACY?

Teaching generic strategies in content area literacy, like those discussed above, are only one path toward greater comprehension of academic text. Proponents of disciplinary literacy explain that when students read content area texts well, they read them the same way the experts in that discipline read them. For example, biology students should read text in the same way biologists read text. Foundationally, disciplinary reading is the belief that each discipline carries with it a unique set of language structures, methods of communicating, fundamental purposes, and specific genres (Shanahan & Shanahan, 2012). Teachers look to the leaders in the field of study to determine appropriate strategies for making sense of text within that field. When compared to content area literacy, disciplinary literacy is an emerging way of thinking about reading for meaning. Consequently, researchers and teachers alike are sharing new insights and strategies to help students read like historians, mathematicians, scientists, or literary experts.

With regard to reading, one of the most fundamental differences in the disciplines is the purpose for reading (Shanahan & Shanahan, 2012). Historians—and student readers of history—usually read from multiple sources in order to piece together the most complete and accurate picture of historical events. They use the context in which the text was written as a lens through which to view the information. Scientists—and student readers of science texts — evaluate information, but they have a dedicated focus on data analysis. Mathematicians—and student readers of mathematics—read to uncover and extend logical reasoning and numerical patterns. Literary scholars—and student readers of literature—interpret language, history, and human nature.

The following table provides examples of discipline-specific purposes for reading.

Social Studies	Science	Mathematics	English Language Arts
analyze primary sources	evaluate information	ascertain how mathematic algorithms relate to procedure	analyze author's point of view
determine bias	interpret descriptions of data	identify extraneous information in word problems	evaluate literary quality
analyze the relevance of the source to a particular argument	critique/support hypotheses using data	identify the correct algorithm for each word problem	interpret printed works

19. WHAT STRATEGIES SHOULD I USE DURING THE READ SECTION?

Unfortunately, the reading and thinking process that occurs in each student's brain is invisible to teachers. Then how is it possible to know if students are really thinking? Most of us have probably taught several students who are very skilled at "fake reading." This is precisely why providing the class with a specific process to hold their thinking while reading comes into play. Here are three strategies to ensure that students are thinking while reading rather than just pretending to be engaged in the reading process. These strategies can be used in isolation or in combination with each other. Each of the strategies accomplishes three important goals: they naturally slow down the reading process; they promote active reading; and they improve future writing. Above all, they give student readers dedicated practice in meeting the goals of both content area and disciplinary literacy.

> *Top Three Strategies* to Ensure Active Reading:
> *1. Pay Attention To List (PAT List)*
> *2. Annotation*
> *3. Highlighting PLUS*

1. Pay Attention To List (PAT List)

This strategy is for teachers who like to be in charge of the classroom. It is for those who worry that students might not glean all they need when reading the text independently. A Pay Attention to List is a way for teachers to guide student thinking with discipline-specific directions as they read independently. The PAT List gives students a concrete way to think like a scientist, historian, mathematician, or literary expert. With a PAT List, one can imagine a miniature teacher sitting on each student's shoulder...right next to his/her ear. The teacher whispers, "Hey, slow down, this is a really important part."

When using PAT Lists with students, the teacher previews the text ahead of the lesson to determine the words, phrases, sentences, or paragraphs that she wants students to pay close attention to. She creates a list of those items so that students can reference them while reading. The PAT List can be as generic or detailed as the teacher wants, but each item on the list should help students accomplish the learning goal for that day.

Sounds like...

- *As you read this chapter, I'd like for you to pay close attention to the terms I've listed on the smart board. When you come across these items in the text, slow down, take notes, and reread, if necessary, to ensure that you understand them.*

- *Use your PAT handout to guide your thinking while you read this article. On it I've selected several quotations from the reading that are significant to understanding our content objective.*

- *When you encounter the ideas listed on the Pay Attention To List, please record some evidence of your thinking about that idea. Remember, you have your list of stems in the front of your journal to help you.*

Examples

2nd grade Reading

PAT List: **Character Response**

Pay attention to

1. Kimberly's actions
2. Feeling words

5th grade Social Studies

PAT List: Pay attention to

- How we acquired the land (was it through an agreement, a battle/war, purchase, or some other way)
- Where the land was located
- Which acquistion you think was most important

 *Examples:*

7th grade Math

PAT List: **Probability**

Probability • Outcome • Sample space
Simple event • Complementary event
How to determine fairness

High School World Geography

PAT List: **Push/Pull Factors**

- On page 342, read the third paragraph slowly. It gives you an outline for the rest of the reading.
- On page 343, read the first two paragraphs. Note three reasons that make economic push factors significant.
- On page 343, look at the migration graph. This is a great visual summary of paragraph four.
- On page 344, read the second paragraph. Can you imagine living through that? What would you have done?
- On page 344, read paragraphs 3-5. You can skim this section because it is a review of what we talked about last week.
- On page 344, read paragraph six. Reread this paragraph to ensure you understand it. It summarizes the essential ideas related to push/pull factors.

High School Science

PAT List: **Biomolecules**

- 2 reasons why carbon is important
- For protein, carbohydrates, lipids, and nucleic acid:
  - Name of subunits
  - Give at least 2 functions
  - At least 1 example

10th grade English

PAT List: **Persuasion/Argument**

- 3 types of appeals
- The difference between persuasion and argument
- Features of an effective appeal

2. Annotation

Annotation is a very common reading, note-taking strategy that has been effective for a long time (Adler, 1940). Annotation gives students practice using all of the general reading strategies that content area literacy promotes because it provides open-ended ways for students to respond to text. Annotation helps readers stay engaged with difficult text. It also helps them make sense of sophisticated wording. In order for students to annotate successfully, they must understand the purpose of annotating. Students need to know that it helps them stay focused, and it helps them understand their reading. Teachers must clearly communicate the reasons students need to take notes while reading; otherwise, annotation becomes meaningless busywork.

 Example

Teacher: You are going to be reading a great deal in my class. Despite my best efforts, I imagine there may be parts of the reading assignments that you may not like for one reason or another. Every reading assignment, however, will have a very important purpose. The purpose is to help you learn concepts that will make you successful in this class and in others. When you read, I am going to ask you to annotate the text. In other words, this means that you are going to take notes while you read. Let's talk about taking notes. What do you think taking notes means?

Student: Like writing stuff on the side.

Teacher: Okay, but what kind of "stuff" should we write?

Student: New words, or you know, stuff.

Teacher: I think that most of you have taken notes in other classes, and you know that it should look like some words on the side of the text or in your journal. But good notes are more than just words on the side of a page, and they serve a very special purpose. Good notes help you stay focused, especially when you are reading something that is difficult or not especially interesting. When you slow down enough to write a note every few para-graphs, it gives your brain time to think about what you are reading, and it helps you make sense of the text.

Teacher: Now, I'm going back to my original question. What kind of "stuff" should you be writing when you take notes? The easy answer is to write down anything that helps you accomplish your purpose for reading the assignment. For example, if your purpose for reading the first three pages of Chapter 7 is to explain how to simplify fractions, then you might: jot down the steps for simplifying fractions as you read them; write a question about one of the steps that is confusing to you; or make a note that says, "These two sentences are really helpful." You can think of note taking as evidence; it means that you are making sense of what you are reading. It is a way to communicate the thoughts you have when you read. I have a chart to show some different ways to annotate a text. This is not a complete list because annotating means writing down anything that will help you accomplish your purpose for reading. This is just a sample of some ways to annotate. I will read it with you, and we will discuss each one.

Types of Notes	Examples
Paraphrase – write the idea in your own words.	"So it says when I divide by the number, I can't have any extras."
Question – ask a question about a confusing part.	"IDK the greatest common factor. What does GCF mean?"
Inference – make a claim based on information from the text.	"This would be faster if I knew my times tables better."
Connect – form a link to something you already know.	"I just thought of when my brother sorts my dad's coins. It always had to be equal."
Comment – write notes as if you were having a conversation with the author.	"I wish you put more examples right here. This is not enough."

An introductory lesson like the one described in the example will help students and teachers alike read with greater attention and comprehension of the text. Whenever teachers read aloud during class, the thinking can be made visible to students by annotating. Model this kind of thinking as often as possible with texts of any length. Whether annotating a word problem or a PowerPoint slide with text, both give the opportunity to show students how to think through the reading. This process makes comprehension transparent, concrete, and reproducible.

There are two common pitfalls related to annotation: students copying parts of the text, word for word, or students writing notes like, "Huh?" "IDK!" or "I don't get this." Notes of this kind do little to help students gain deeper understanding. One way to avoid these pitfalls is to acknowledge their existence, explain why they are ineffective notes, and then provide an alternative.

 *Example:*

Teacher: I've noticed several sets of notes that say, "Huh?" or "IDK." I don't think those kinds of notes are very helpful, and here's why: We write notes to help us make sense of what we are reading. If I write IDK and then keep reading, that does not help me understand any better. I just stay confused. Here is an alternative: Next time you don't understand something and are tempted to write "Huh?" or "I don't get this," try to imagine that you have an expert sitting right next to you who knows all the answers. What could you ask that person to help you clear up your confusion? The question that you would ask is what you should write...instead of "Huh?" For instance, you might ask: Why does the author think it is important to include this detail? What is the author trying to tell me? Then, you can either reread or continue reading with a focus in mind. This will help you find the answers to your questions. Then you will be able to make sense of what you are reading.

Another consideration related to annotation is frequency. How many notes should students record for any given reading assignment? There is no magic ratio for numbers of pages/paragraphs read to number of annotations made, but students often need a frame of reference. Students do not need to annotate every sentence because they will never finish reading, nor should they speed through an entire text without recording any notes. So how many notes should students take? That depends. Here are some factors to consider:

1. The purpose for the reading.

Remember, annotation is a way to help students accomplish the purpose. Some purposes are very straightforward while others may be deep and complex. For example, let's say the class is reading an article about biodiversity. Consider these two different purposes for reading the same article:

Purpose #1: to explain the terms biodiversity, ecosystems, and climate
Purpose #2: to analyze how biodiversity affects a community's stability

To accomplish purpose #1, students would probably only need to make notes in the three areas where those terms are defined. To accomplish purpose #2, however, students may need to annotate at the end of each paragraph, or more, to fully develop their thinking.

2. The complexity of the text.

The more difficult the text, the more often students should slow down to record their thinking.

3. The reader.

Some students like to write and rely heavily on notes as a way to process information. Other students view note taking as an impediment to reading, and they prefer not to slow down. Some students struggle with putting their thoughts into words while others can do it with ease.

After considering each of the above factors for any given reading assignment, the teacher can offer an appropriate expectation for how frequently students should annotate while reading text. As students become more comfortable and skilled when annotating, they can independently determine the right amount of notes to take to accomplish their purpose for reading.

3. Highlighting PLUS

Highlighters and students can be a very bright combination. However, when asked to highlight important parts of a text, students often fall victim to over-highlighting. Highlighting PLUS greatly curtails students' willingness to over-mark a text because it requires them to highlight plus explain anything they highlight, either in written or oral form. This holds students accountable because they need to have a specific reason for each phrase, sentence, or section they highlight. To begin Highlighting PLUS, the teacher asks students to highlight (or underline or copy into a journal) parts of the text based on specific criteria, such as phrases that support the purpose for reading. As students read and encounter those phrases, they highlight them. This puts the spotlight on the reading purpose over and over again. While reading or later in the lesson, students return to each highlighted section and add their thinking. Then students meet with a partner/group to defend or explain their notes, or they can record their reasons for highlighting in a journal. Much like annotation, it is helpful to provide students with a range of expectation such as, "Please highlight between 3-5 ideas while reading." The teacher has complete flexibility to set the standard for what (words, phrases, sentences, etc.) and how much to highlight. Teachers can choose to focus on general reading strategies that support content area literacy, or they can focus on ways of processing the text to support disciplinary literacy. Highlighting PLUS is particularly helpful when reading requires students to connect ideas from many parts of the text to accomplish a reading goal.

 *Example:*

Teacher: Today you are going to read Martin Luther King Jr.'s "I Have a Dream" speech. Your purpose for reading is to explain the impact his speech had on the Civil Rights Movement. While you read and think about the impact of the speech, please highlight the statements or phrases that you think were the most persuasive or influential to his audience. You must highlight at least three items. Remember, after reading you will need to explain why you selected those items in your journal. Be selective in your choices.

20. HOW DO I HELP INCREASE READING STAMINA?

We are most familiar with the concept of stamina in the world of sports. It is the ability to sustain the physical and mental efforts to accomplish the task. Stamina is an important consideration in the classroom as well. Just as a runner builds his physical stamina by increasing the distance and speed he runs, so must students build reading stamina by increasing the length and complexity of the text they read. The runner does not begin by running a marathon; students should not be expected to begin by reading a long, dense text. The goal is to build student reading stamina over time. Teachers can begin with short simple texts and increase the length and complexity of the text as stamina increases.

Reading stamina is a topic to be discussed with students. Let them in on the game, too. Instead of thinking, "How can I get them to read this?" open the discussion to the class. It might sound like this, "At the end of this unit I want everyone to be able to read and understand _____. It is two pages long and loaded with academic terminology. What kinds of practice do you think you will need in order to be really comfortable reading this?" Brief discussions of this nature clearly communicate the high expectations you have for all students when they are reading challenging text assigned in class. It also requires students to take ownership of their learning because they see that the teacher will not do everything for them. While the teacher will support them, the student can and should do the work independently.

21. WHAT DO I DO WHILE STUDENTS ARE READING?

Imagine you have created a well-planned lesson, and after setting a clear purpose for reading, you have told them they have 15 minutes to read a short text. Your students are settled into make sense of the text and the room is quiet. This moment can sometimes feel awkward. You might start thinking about all of the content you still have left to teach. You might wish that they'd hurry up and finish so that you aren't running behind schedule. You begin to worry that they might not glean all of the important content while reading on their own. These thoughts are common and perfectly normal. While students are reading, we can use that time to great effect if we are prepared. Here are some ideas for ways to fully utilize your time while students are reading:

1. Monitor students' comprehension. There are several ways to accomplish this.

"Sprinkling the love" This refers to when a teacher walks the room intentionally checking that each student is actively reading. Moving about the room helps to minimize off-task behavior, but it should go deeper than that. The goal of this technique is not only to make sure students appear to be reading, but also to actually read their annotations on the text, notice what they are marking/highlighting, and read their facial expressions. We use the reading time to provide "spot checks" with various students, giving them brief and specific feedback based on their notes or reading habits.

"Air dropping the love" This refers to giving a specific student dedicated focus during the reading time. The teacher sits with that student and guides his/her comprehension in an effort to give him or her a large amount of individualized support so that the student can be more independently successful when reading future texts.

2. Pull a small group. Teachers can select specific students to meet with him or her during the reading time. This small group might read the text together to ensure comprehension, or the teacher might have an alternative goal for the group. Working on a specific skill, reteaching previous content, and previewing upcoming content are some examples of how the teacher can differentiate instruction with the small group.

3. Model your comprehension of the text. While students are reading, the teacher reads the same text silently using a document camera. Students can observe the teacher's annotations while they read. Providing this real-time model is especially helpful for students who struggle with comprehension or are prone to distraction while reading.

4. Provide positive reinforcement and encouragement in writing. This idea came from a teacher who walks throughout her classroom with a Post-it notepad and pen in hand. She uses the reading time to write and give students "happy notes." Many times the written comments are direct responses to the "thinking" that students have put on their text. She validates their use of reading strategies or encourages their responses to the text. She also uses the "happy notes" as a way to build positive relationships, in particular with students who are apathetic toward reading or have behavioral challenges in class.

5. Reread the text with intention. Teachers can read the text themselves in order to move through the lesson with greater intention. Having the text fresh in mind can help the teacher anticipate challenges, generate thoughtful follow-up questions, and become better prepared to facilitate student conversations during Talk #2.

6. Minimize vocabulary barriers. Create a way for students to seek help for unknown words or difficult sections of text while they are reading. One teacher has a set of blue highlighters on each table. When students encounter an unknown word, they use the blue highlighter to mark it. While the teacher monitors the class, if she sees something highlighted in blue on a text, she checks in with that student to clarify his/her understanding. This technique is especially helpful for students who lack confidence or do not prefer to raise their hand for help. It allows them to remain more anonymous but still get the support they need. Another variation of this technique is to give each student a blank Post-it. They can place the Post-it on a specific part of the desk, say top right, whenever they need teacher support. Circling unknown words is also effective.

7. Prepare the next part of the lesson. Teachers can use reading time to prepare, pass out, or collect materials or resources for the next part of the lesson. Handing out envelopes with discussion questions, pulling up a slide with discussion stems, and posting anchor charts that will support student writing are some examples of ways to prepare the next part of the lesson.

8. Stop talking. A silent classroom is sometimes unsettling to the teacher; it is easy to fall victim to restating directions, adding additional thoughts, prompting the class, etc. Once we have given clear directions and allowed students to begin reading, however, we must stay quiet so they can actually read.

Overview of READ	Strategies
PAT List	• Create a list of significant words, phrases, or ideas from the text. • Ask students to use that list while reading to ensure they understand important concepts.
Annotation	• Directly teach students ways to annotate. • Ask students to annotate while reading so they have a record of their thinking.
Highlighting PLUS	• Ask students to highlight important ideas from the text. • Give students the opportunity to refer to their highlighted text after reading, and have them explain why they highlighted it.

CAMPUS CONNECTIONS

1. As a team, how can teachers plan to have students read in class?

2. What adjustments are needed to ensure that all students can and do read the text?

3. What are the pros/cons of transcribing lectures into texts for students to read?

4. What resources can teams use to find appropriate texts for upcoming units of study?

5. What is the difference between content area literacy and disciplinary literacy?

Practice

1. With a partner, transcribe an upcoming lecture (direct teach) into written form for students to read.

2. With your team, create 2-3 PAT Lists for upcoming units.

CHAPTER FOUR
Talk #2

This step is similar to Talk #1 because it creates opportunities for student conversation. It engages, or in some cases, re-engages students with the academic concept of the lesson. Conversation provides students with a much-needed opportunity to process the information they encountered during reading. It also gives them a chance to hear other students' perspectives on a topic. There is a significant amount of intrinsic motivation embedded in Talk #2 because students want to talk with each other. Facilitating targeted and effective conversations, however, can be difficult.

One of the greatest gifts you can give your students is the set of skills needed to productively collaborate with others.

−J. Zweirs

22. WHAT IS TALK #2?

Talk #2 consists of small groups of students talking with each other for the purpose of clarifying concepts and deepening understanding of the lesson content. The conversation is the bridge from one independent activity (reading the text) to a second independent activity (writing a response). More specifically, the goals of Talk #2 are to use conversation to process the text and prepare for writing. During this step, students get the chance to compare their understanding of the text with other students. They also gain and develop new ideas from their peers that can only help improve their written responses. Just as the text should tightly align with the content objective of the lesson, so should the conversation in Talk #2. Crafting questions that require students to return to the text for essential understanding takes some time and thought, but constructed questioning is the key component to shape an effective conversation.

✔ TALK #2 is	✘ TALK #2 is NOT
shared responsibility among all students.	individuals working on separate tasks within the same group.
supported by clear expectations.	delivering ambiguous directions such as, "Go to your groups and discuss Chapter 8."
well-paced, most often brief (1-10 minutes).	extended dialogue.*
small groups of students (2-4) discussing content concepts.	just retelling basic facts, knowledge, or memorization.
non-threatening exposure to new terms/ideas.	whole class discussion.

As students gain skill in academic communication, they may want and even require extended amounts of time to process the text and prepare to write. Extended dialogue is recommended only when the dialogue produces new insights and deeper levels of understanding.

23. WHAT STRATEGIES CAN I USE FOR TALK #2?

There are two basic ways to conduct Talk #2: teacher-created conversation and student-created conversation. In the first approach, the teacher determines the focus of student talk by providing a thought-provoking question to discuss. The second approach allows students to determine the nature of the conversation. These two approaches can be conducted in the following ways:

1. Envelope, Please!
(Teacher-created conversation)

To conduct a teacher-created conversation, the teacher writes a question on a piece of paper and places it in an envelope. This creates a little drama and a sense of anticipation for the upcoming conversation. He hands one envelope to each group and lets the groups discuss the answer. The envelopes can contain more than one discussion question, a different question for each group, or an identical question for all groups.

The success or failure of the student conversation in this activity is largely determined by the question itself. A question whose answer is straightforward and obvious will generate, at most, a short and dull conversation. A question that "calls for comparison or invites evaluation or judgment," however, can lead to a much more lively and interesting conversation (Probst, 2007). Additionally, "questions that bring the text and the students' lives together are likely to lead the class both to impassioned discussion of the issues raised by the text and to telling their own stories, stories you might otherwise never hear," (Probst, 2007).

So how do teachers write questions that will ensure high-quality conversations? Zwiers and Crawford (2011) provide three guiding questions for teachers to ask when planning student conversation:

1. Does the question connect the current text to the essential understandings (big ideas) of the unit?

2. Does the question leave room for multiple perspectives, abstract ideas, and negotiation of meanings?

3. Is the question one you would like to talk about with your friends or colleagues?

24. Why engage in TALK #2?

Conversations are a fundamental part of the human experience, primarily because we learn so much by talking and listening to others (Ezzedeen, 2008). Research supports the fact that when students engage with each other in meaningful conversations, the results are often beyond the abilities of individual students within the group (Wertsch, del Rio, & Alvarez, 1995). The act of collaborating with others, particularly after reading, actually improves comprehension of the text (Gallagher, 2004). There are several reasons for this. First, students have an opportunity to compare their understanding with others. Second, students look at the text from diverse perspectives. Third, students have the opportunity to clarify and verify information.

Having consistent opportunities to dialogue about the text increases students' future engagement during independent reading tasks. Because students anticipate group conversation with their peers, they tend to pay closer attention as they are reading (Hoyt, 1999).

Talk #2 occurs at a critical point within the lesson—just after a reading task and just before a writing task. Talk #2 not only supports deeper reading, but it also increases the likelihood of more effective writing. In a sense, it is a rehearsal for the writing students are about to do. During Talk #2, students discuss their findings with others and make connections to the reading. When we allow students to talk with one another, we undoubtedly improve their reading comprehension and prepare them for written communication.

Let's look at each question in a little more detail.

Does the question connect the current text to the essential understandings (big ideas) of the unit? The sheer volume of standards and content for which teachers are responsible requires that not a minute of class time be wasted. Conversations must propel students toward mastery of those standards. The question, then, should require students to revisit the text for support for their thinking. If they do not need the text in order to have the discussion, the question is not well aligned, and the ensuing conversation will likely run off course.

Does the question leave room for multiple perspectives, abstract ideas, and negotiation of meanings? The only way a conversation can move from a quick regurgitation of information to a rich academic dialogue is if some "mental wrestling" is required. Conversation prompts must require students to think for themselves as well as to navigate the thoughts of others. Often, teachers believe that students just need to know the content, but there is so much more they need to know. Students need to be able to deepen and develop content understanding as well. When offering a question that asks students to wrestle with an essential understanding, the teacher has the chance to determine whether students have the base content knowledge they need for a substantial and measurable response.

Is the question one you would like to talk about with your friends or colleagues? This thought is a litmus test that can be applied to every question we put in the envelope. Let's be honest, most students are not going to turn cartwheels with excitement over most academically related conversations, nor will they have a burning desire to talk with their friends in the hallway about their lessons. Often classroom conversations fail because the task is unappealing, drab, or an obvious search for the "right" answer. Essentially, the question really boils down to authenticity. Does the question communicate respect for the learner as a capable thinker? Is it engaging enough to be worthy of precious class time?

Sounds like...

- *How can an algebraic expression help you solve real-world problems?*
- *What are some of the positive and negative impacts of non-renewable energy?*
- *In what ways did the early Egyptian civilization influence the development of the classical civilizations?*
- *How do the characters and events in the novel reflect real people and world events?*
- *If you were the main character, what would you do differently?*

2. Check-in Conversation
(Student-created conversation)

The alternative to teacher-created conversation is to allow students' thoughts, questions, confusions, annotations, and knowledge of the upcoming writing task to drive the discussion. This approach is more flexible and open-ended than the teacher-created conversation. During a Check-in Conversation, students use the talking time to "check-in" with each other about their understanding of the text. While conversing, they can clarify confusing parts, paraphrase essential ideas, evaluate/comment on content, and ask questions. For check-ins to work well, students should use their annotations from the reading to drive the discussion. Referring back to their annotations, students have a starting point for discussion as well as a bank of other comments to use if the dialogue stalls. (There is an interesting and beneficial side effect of Check-in Conversations. After participating in a few of them, students begin to write better annotations when they read text. Working in groups gives students a very real audience for their annotations. As they read the next text, their annotations become more articulate, more detailed, and more insightful.) Once students fully debrief their understanding of the text, they can also use the Check-in Conversation to brainstorm ideas for the upcoming writing task. It can be helpful to provide the writing assignment before Talk time because it gives students an end goal to work toward. It is in this conversation that students hear different perspectives on the same topic, and this will enable them to increase the quality of their written responses.

 Example:

Teacher: We are about to start our Check-in Conversations. Remember, this is the time to draw on the expertise of your group so that you are confident and knowledgeable about the information on pages 76-79. Don't forget to bring the notes from your Pay Attention To List to guide the group discussion.

As you check in with your group, be sure that each person makes at least one comment or asks one question about the reading before brainstorming the reasons for your claim statement.

Okay, class, your groups have seven minutes to discuss words, sentences, sections, or ideas from the reading. You can also use this time to talk about which textual evidence you are going to include in the short answer you will write at the close of this conversation.

25. HOW CAN I REALLY MAKE STUDENT CONVERSATION WORK?

I have given many classes the opportunity for group discussion, only for it to result in abysmal failure. Upon reflecting on those "collaborations," there were some recurring obstacles. Some kids do all the work, some are off task, and some do not participate at all. Collaborative tasks have common roadblocks that result in low-quality student conversation. Unfortunately, some students are not nearly as skilled in conversation as teachers are, so they must be taught. The most effective solution for low-quality student conversation is to "name the elephant in the (class)room." In other words, directly address the obvious problem you anticipate before putting students to task within their groups. We want to set students up for success, and the way to accomplish that is to troubleshoot difficulties ahead of time.

Steps for Addressing Challenges to High-Quality Conversation

Step	Description	Sounds Like
Step One: Identify the problem.	Name the specific barriers that are getting in the way when students try to have a high-quality conversation. Directly state the anticipated problem and provide examples.	• *I've noticed that when you work in a group...* • *I observed something in the last class period that I want to eliminate from our group conversations...* • *Some of you are... For example...*
Step Two: Show students what to do.	Name and model the desired outcome/behavior. Directly state expectations and provide examples.	• *When you are with your group, I should see...* • *If another student _____, an excellent response is...* • *Always _____. For example...*
Step Three: Explain why students should do it.	State the significance of meeting expectations.	• *The reason I ask you to _____ is...* • *_____ is significant because...* • *When you _____, it helps you to...*
Step Four: Observe students.	During student conversations, actively monitor for the presence or absence of the desired behavior. Provide specific and timely feedback related to the observations.	• *I just heard you _____. That is exactly what I was talking about during our earlier discussion.* • *Remember what we discussed in... It...* • *I can tell that your group really understands how to _____ because I saw each of you...*

 *Example:*

Teacher: I've noticed students who sit back, draw, or check their phones underneath the desks while they are supposed to be working in groups. *(Identify the problem.)*

When you are with your group, I should see you looking at the speaker, and I should hear you contributing to the conversation. If you aren't sure what to say, you can always ask a question. For example, "Henry, can you tell me more about why you think…?" *(Show students what to do.)*

The reason I ask everyone to contribute is because I know that collaborating with your peers will help you better understand your reading, and it will help you mentally prepare for your writing task. *(Explain why students should do it.)*

When I observe you working in groups, I should see you actively contributing to the group, and I should see that your group understands the assignment. Based on what I see, I will be better able to help you when you are having difficulty. *(Explain the student behavior you observe.)*

26. WHAT ARE FIVE PRIMARY CONSIDERATIONS FOR SUCCESSFUL STUDENT CONVERSATION?

When students successfully engage in academic conversations with their peers, such conversations have strong evidence of the following five features:
- Accountability
- Respect
- Purpose
- Momentum
- Academic tone

Conversely, when conversations are unsuccessful, the root cause can usually be linked to a breakdown in one or more of these considerations.

Accountability: The Little Red Hen Effect is alive and well.

As the story goes, the Little Red Hen asks all her friends for help while gathering the ingredients to make and bake bread. No one is willing to pitch in until the bread is ready, and then all of her friends can't wait to help eat it. In many student groups, there is a "Little Red Hen" (or two), who does all the talking (and thinking) and several who, like Little Red's friends, are unwilling to participate in the conversation. But, they are happy to receive a good grade for the work.

Tips for Accountability:

- Structure the conversation so that each person has a job/role/focus (For example: focuser, leader, praise-giver, etc.)

- Give individual assessment (feedback, comments, grades, etc.) in addition to group assessment.

- Role-play to highlight the feelings of various group members when one person doesn't contribute.

- Create a rubric for students to grade each other's participation/contribution.

- Give each member a set number of objects (paper clips, poker chips, counters, etc.) When a group member participates, he puts one of his objects in the center. The goal is for each group member to make at least as many contributions as he has number of objects. This can work in reverse as well. All objects are in the center and group members collect an object for each contribution they make. (Adapted from Kagan, 1994.)

- Provide groups questions or sentence stems for how they can participate even if they are confused or do not have anything new to say. (For example: "I'm confused. Can someone explain _____?," or "One reason I agree with _____ is because…")

- Strategically group students. It is sometimes helpful to put all of the "Little Red Hens" in one group, and likewise, put all of the more reticent speakers in another group. This allows you to work with the quieter group in order to increase their oral communication skills.

Respect: With friends like that, who needs enemies?

Students can be hard on each other, often saying thoughtless, yet hurtful words, or acting in a joking, yet disrespectful manner. Creating a respectful classroom culture is a common goal for all teachers. It takes constant monitoring and sometimes swift action to curtail rude comments and disruptive/offensive behavior. The challenge of maintaining a respectful environment is compounded during small group collaboration because students are on their own while the teacher moves from group to group to offer feedback. Without respect, the group can become frustrating, risky, and even unsafe for its members.

Tips for Respect:

- Establish norms for respect such as, "You do not have to agree with every-one, but you do have to listen to their ideas." Or, "Be open-minded."

- Model respect and share real-life examples that show how to act in a respectful way. (Example: replying to a bossy email, handling a rude customer in a store, responding to an offensive comment, etc.)

- Communicate zero tolerance for acting or speaking in a disrespectful way.

- Have individual groups create "Group Norms," a collective agreement iden-tifying acceptable behavior within that group.

- Model examples and non-examples of specific group interactions.

- Assign a group member the task of addressing disrespect. In one class I've observed, they call this the role of "Referee." This person should be selected with intention by the teacher.

- Create a word or phrase for group members to use when they experience or observe disrespect occurring. The use of the "safeword" allows all mem-bers to quickly reflect and adjust their behavior, facial expressions, and comments without any specific student being singled out.

- If you witness disrespect, address it in a reflective and solution-oriented way, such as, "How can we handle this next time?"

Purpose: Two heads are better than one.

Students often view academic tasks, even interactive tasks like group discussion, much the same way I view housecleaning tasks: finish it as quickly as possible; it doesn't have to be perfect, just passable. Even when students are actively engaged, the discussion centers on coming up with "the right answer" rather than generating and extending various thoughts about the topic. Students can often be blind to the power of collaboration; many times they do not see the benefits of sharing ideas to develop better understanding. It is also easy for students, growing up in the age of instant gratification, to quickly get off topic. One tangential comment can derail an entire group.

Tips for Purpose:

- Directly teach the purpose of collaboration.

- Clearly articulate the specific purpose for each conversation.

- Provide cues for students to stay on (or get back on) topic during discussion. (Example: "So, John was explaining…" or "Let's look at our task again.")

- Acknowledge and value divergent thinking or diverse solutions.

- Offer feedback that encourages deep and wide thinking rather than a search for correct answers. (Example: "What else…?")

- One teacher keeps a basket of legos at the center of each group's table. When a group member offers a new idea, she gets to stack a lego. As more ideas surface, the lego "tower" gets larger and larger. This teacher also explained that groups became competitive to see who could create the tallest tower, which also equated to the largest set of different ideas.

Momentum: Keep the ball rolling.

Student conversations are sometimes over before they begin because the group members do not have any momentum behind their thinking. They are not sure what to say. In other groups, the conversation begins well but then loses momentum before the topic has been fully discussed. Students struggle with how to initiate dialogue as well as how to sustain it.

Tips for Momentum:

- Teach students gestures that cue the speaker to elaborate, such as pointing to the text to ask for evidence or pretending to stretch a rubber band to ask for more information about the topic.

- Provide sentence stems and questions that will help students if they get stuck, such as, "Tell me more about…" or "How did you decide…?"

- Role play a conversation that lacks momentum, and ask students to suggest how to get it going again. Post their responses so that groups can use those ideas as a resource.

- Use "stay or stray" strategy. After a couple of minutes, move 1-2 group members to another group. Now each group has some "old" and some "new" members for continuing the dialogue.

- Ask members to paraphrase the previous speaker's idea before adding their own idea. This has the added bonus of slowing down the conversation so that all members stay "up to speed" as well as increasing listener accountability.

Tone: Talk like the experts

Students often think the language used in content area classrooms is strange and incomprehensible. To them, it is almost as if the classes are being taught in a foreign language. They are unfamiliar with, and uncomfortable using, academic terminology. When we ask students to talk, therefore, they usually communicate in the way in which they feel most comfortable. They interact using short phrases, general terminology, slang, one-word responses, or text message type abbreviations. Engaging in conversation about an academic topic without using academic language hinders students from gaining fluency and deeper understanding of academic concepts.

Tips for Tone:

- Create norms for communicating "as if you are the teacher" or "like the expert."

- Provide linguistic supports to students. For example, provide: word walls, sentence stems, or lists of relevant academic terms to use during the discussion process.

- Model responses that have a casual/social tone, and restate them using an academic tone. Ask students to do the same.

- Emphasize students speaking in complete sentences, during Talk #2 and throughout all other class time.

- Give each group a prop that can help to cue them to speak in an academic way. Some examples include a microphone, a pair of fake glasses, or a lab coat. The goal is that groups see and use a physical object that will help them remember to communicate more formally.

Overview of TALK #2	Strategies
Envelope, Please!	• Create 1-3 open-ended questions related to the text. • Give student groups open-ended questions in an envelope. • Ask groups to discuss answers to questions.
Check-in Conversation	• Give student groups an opportunity to discuss their annotations from the text. • Give student groups an opportunity to brainstorm ideas for writing.

CAMPUS CONNECTIONS

Discuss

1. How can the team use the information from "Five Considerations for Successful Student Conversation" to better support students?

_____

_____

2. How can the team eliminate or minimize the reservations we have about students talking in class?

_____

_____

3. What do students need in order to conduct a Check-in Conversation in the classroom?

_____

_____

4. What is the value of having students talk with each other after reading and before writing?

_____

_____

Practice

1. Write 1-3 discussion questions for an upcoming unit of study. (See pp.57-58 for reference.)

_____

_____

CHAPTER FIVE
Write

Being able to control words in writing literally means having the power to change the world. Think of Abraham Lincoln's "Gettysburg Address," Martin Luther King Jr.'s "I Have a Dream" speech, or Ralph Waldo Emerson's "Self-Reliance." Of course, students in all grades have to practice constantly to achieve such command of language. That's why it is important for teachers to provide regular opportunities for students to engage in authentic writing tasks. As students practice the art of writing, they gain many advantages. Not only do they have the chance to process and reflect on their understanding of content, but they learn to express their thoughts, advocate for themselves, and use their words to influence others. When they become strong and fluent writers, students become articulate members of a larger world.

Writing, to me, is simply thinking through my fingers. –Isaac Asimov

27. WHAT IS WRITE?

During the Write section of a TRTW lesson, students communicate their understanding of the content objective in writing. Consider this step a window into student thinking and a concrete product of the lesson.

✔ The WRITE Section **is**	✘ The WRITE Section **is NOT**
students generating their own thoughts.	copying notes or information from resources.
students writing to make a compelling argument or to explain a topic fully.	one word responses, fill in the blank, or a series of questions.
students writing complete thoughts/sentences.	students recording fragments or bulleted lists.

28. WHAT DO STUDENTS WRITE?

The content objective should always drive the writing task. Writing, like reading, takes valuable time; therefore, it is critical that the task focuses directly on the essential understandings of the academic concept. The majority of writing that occurs in a content area classroom, with the exception of an English language arts class, is expository in nature. In math, science, and social studies, students write to inform, explain, and prove academic concepts. Therefore, two significant forms of student writing are: clear explanations and compelling arguments. For most lessons, the writing task will take the shape of a short answer response or a student-generated paragraph that clearly articulates understanding. In the case of early elementary classrooms, the writing might take the shape of a visual representation or a simplified response, and may also need to be guided by the teacher.

29. HOW DO I TEACH STUDENTS TO WRITE?

Asking students to explain their thinking in writing can result in great frustration for students as well as teachers. Students are often apprehensive about the quality of their writing skills, and teachers see that students are unsuccessful when they write. Many students come to us with significant background in writing due in large part to our English language arts curriculum. However, many science, social studies, and math teachers often hear their students say, "But we're not in English class," when they are asked to write. Teachers explain that their students only connect the task of writing with English language arts, where they generally learn grammar, spelling, mechanics, and literary responses. They perceive math class as a place to solve problems, science class as a place to conduct experiments, and history class as a place to learn facts about the past. They compartmentalize their learning into discrete sections, and they rarely transfer the skills they learned in one class to another class. An interview I conducted with two high school teachers clearly demonstrates this phenomenon. For example:

> *An English III and a U.S. History teacher were discussing a student they had in common. The U.S. History teacher was lamenting about how poorly this student was performing on the short answer portion of the assessments. The English III teacher double-checked the last name of the student to confirm they were talking about the same young man. She was dumbfounded because he was one of the strongest writers in all of her classes. When they compared the same student's written work, both teachers were left speechless. The U.S. History teacher was blown away by the student's clear communication skills and precise word choice in his English paper. In history class, these skills were undeniably absent. After reviewing the short answer response from the history class, the English teacher said, in a deflated voice, "He knows better." This student was obviously not making the writing connection across content areas.*

30. Why WRITE?

Knowing how to write well is critical to student development. The National Commission on Writing acknowledges that students need to work with the details of their reading. In doing so, they learn to make sense of the concepts, they extend their understanding, and they learn to communicate their knowledge to others. Basically, the commission is saying that students learn in more depth as they engage in the act of writing.

Writing gives students the means to measure their understanding of concepts and to extend that understanding (Hoyt, 1999). The writing portion of the TRTW approach directly supports the recommendations of Writing Next, i.e., a meta-analysis of the current research on adolescent literacy for improving academic achievement (Graham & Perin, 2007). Writing Next reported a strong correlation between student success and student ability to summarize, collaborate, and meet specific product goals for writing, all of which are explicitly taught and modeled during the writing portion of a TRTW lesson.

With this story in mind, an observation can be made. Part of any teacher's goal is to help students gain a more global perspective on learning. Students need to see themselves as readers, writers, and problem solvers in every class. To do this is to engage in meta-cognitive thinking. Students need to accomplish a task and then think critically about the steps they took to achieve their goal. If they focus on meta-cognitive thinking, then the transfer of knowledge and skills across the curriculum will become more efficient.

Just as there are strategies that good readers use while reading academic text, there are also a couple of basic considerations that all successful writers keep in mind when writing. As students write, it is important that they remember both the audience and the form.

31. HOW IS AUDIENCE DETERMINED?

All writers must know and think about the audience for whom they are writing. The intended audience for this book, for example, is classroom teachers. I am ever mindful of this targeted group as I write. I am aware that everything I include must pass the "practical application" test in order for my audience to be able to use this resource. If, however, my intended audience were central office program coordinators or educational researchers, for example, both the content and the way in which I communicate it would be very different.

Determining the audience is the most critical factor for student writers to remember when they write. It gives students a clear direction for their writing and an authentic place to return to if they get stuck. A math teacher once told me that the most effective technique she has employed to get her students to clearly explain how they solved their math problems is to ask them to write their explanation "as if your English teacher were going to read it." Why is this so effective for her students? The reason is that she is giving them a very real audience, one they can visualize and one for whom they can anticipate clear expectations. Providing students with an audience can and does result in better writing. Why is this? Students perceive their teachers to be the intellectual authority in the class; the experts in the field, if you will. If the student is writing for an expert who already knows everything (you), then taking shortcuts and omitting details seems appropriate and acceptable. Students think, "Why do I need to explain what each variable represents to Mrs. Nelson? She is the one who taught this to me in the first place. She already knows all that. All I need to do is write the correct answer." Making sure students know their audience helps drive their writing decisions.

Sounds like...

- *Write your opinion as if you are trying to convince your friends to agree that your way of thinking is the right way.*

- *Write your directions so clearly that a class of first graders could follow them easily. Do not leave out any important details.*

- *Explain your answer to me as completely as possible. Try to anticipate every question I might ask you, and answer those questions in your paragraph.*

32. WHY IS IT IMPORTANT TO IDENTIFY THE FORM OF WRITING FOR STUDENTS?

If teachers want students to communicate their thinking in writing successfully, they must be given a clear framework for what that looks like. Naming the form or type of writing expected and giving explicit guidelines for completion minimizes failure. The objective of identifying the writing format is to eliminate the disorganized, stream-of-consciousness responses that so often fill student papers.

There are numerous forms of writing that teachers can model, such as narratives, letters, directions, editorials, poems, plays, recipes, etc. When thinking about the forms of writing that students can use to demonstrate content knowledge, however, we can collapse it down to two: a clear explanation and making a claim with evidence. The next section gives examples of how to create well-written responses.

Sounds like...

- *In your response, clearly explain _____.*

- *Your task is to argue one side of the issue and provide at least three pieces of textual evidence that support your stance.*

- *Write an explanation of your work. Make sure to explain each step in your process.*

K-5

Claim: A butterfly is a living thing.	
❌ **Non-example:** Evidence without reasoning	Butterflies are living things. Living things move.
✅ **Example:** Evidence with reasoning	Butterflies are living things. Living things move. I see butterflies move all around outside.

33. HOW CAN I HELP IMPROVE MY STUDENTS' WRITING?

In my experience, struggling writers have benefitted most when I share an underdeveloped writing sample. Since real writing takes place in the revision process, this step offers the opportunity to walk students through the revision process. As we revise together, the class is able to see how a non-example writing sample can become an effective written response.

 *Example:*

Teacher: Okay, class, let's get started. I know that I normally tell you exactly what I want you to do, and then I usually give you a model of the assignment. Today I thought I would change things just a little bit. Before you begin writing, I want to show you a paragraph that would not receive a passing grade. You are going to help me find all the reasons why it is not a good response, and then we'll fix it together. Remember, in this class, I am looking for writing that uses academic language and a more formal tone that we use in everyday discussion. The reason we are going to analyze a non-example of the assignment is so that you won't make the same mistakes when you write.

Let's look at the Jack and Jill problem you just solved. We all agreed that the game is not fair, based on our probability calculations. Now, let's see the rest of the assignment.

It says, "Explain why this is either a fair game or an unfair game." Think for a minute about how you would explain it. *(The teacher gives students time to think.)*

Everyone look up here at this student's response. *(The teacher reads the response out loud.)*

> Not a fair game. Jill would get more points and that's not fair.
> Jack is 2/5 and Jill is 3/5. If I were playing I would definitely want to be Jill.
> Tiles that don't match win. I'd try to play something else if
> I were Jack cuz he's gonna lose.

Remember that I told you this is a non-example, one that would not receive a passing grade. Why? Turn to your partner and see if you can come up with at least 3 reasons why this response is ineffective. (The teacher gives students 1-2 minutes for discussion.) Okay, bring your conversations to a close, and let's discuss this with the whole group. What did you decide? Yes, Kareem?

Kareem: There are incomplete sentences. It sounds choppy.

Teacher: Yes, that is correct. This response has fragments like, "Not a fair game," and "Tiles that don't match win." A well-written response will be written with complete sentences. Elsa, what did you decide?

Elsa: I think it is kind of like Kareem's. The response sounds like how I would talk, with words like "cuz." We said it should sound more serious, and it shouldn't have slang.

Teacher: Excellent! This response does have a social tone. It sounds like a student talking with his friends. He uses words like "cuz" and "gonna." A well-written response will have an academic tone and should include academic terminology related to the topic. In this case, the response should include terms such as: probability, odds, equally likely, sample space, etc. Who else has an idea? Diego?

Diego: The person who wrote this talks about himself a lot. He says, "I" this and "I" that many times.

Teacher: The writer does include himself in the response using the pronoun "I." A well-written response does not include very many pronouns. Instead, it addresses the topic directly using specific nouns. Great observation! Sara, did you and your partner have any other reasons?

Sara: Yes, we don't think the writer followed directions very well. It says to explain why the game is unfair, and this sample doesn't really explain the reason.

Teacher: I agree. This is an unclear explanation. The response is correct because it says the game is unfair, and it uses the correct fractions for Jack and Jill (2/5 and 3/5, respectively). But, there is no clear explanation for why the game is unfair. The writer did not directly answer the question. A well-written response directly answers the question and provides specific supporting details. Effective responses always follow a logical sequence.

In addition, the use of non-example and example samples helps students identify the characteristics of academic writing they can imitate. Seeing the characteristic (or its absence) in the sample solidifies student understanding because they can identify a non-example academic response, and they can revise it to become an example of academic response. It is a good idea to create an anchor chart during the discussion for students to consult when they write. The anchor chart for the previous discussion might look like this:

Instead of using	Use
fragments	complete sentences
slang and abbreviations	as much academic vocabulary as possible
I, we, you, it	the specific name of the person, place, or thing
disorganized explanations	a logical order, or step-by-step approach

Another benefit of sharing and discussing non-example written responses is that students are often energized by and highly engaged with finding fault in a piece of work that is not their own. They love to pick the response to pieces, and once they have, the door is wide open for the teacher to ask what's wrong with the writing and how they can make it better. This exercise, in and of itself, is one of the best teaching tools. In essence, the students are finding the kind of mistakes they would make in their own papers, and they are thinking of ways to improve them. During this step, students tend to internalize the process of writing and revising. After students have been through the revision steps in class, teachers can and should expect better quality responses from students. Here are some sample paragraphs (both examples and non-examples) for typical writing tasks in each core content area.

K-5 Content Area/ Assignment	✅ Example	❌ Non-example
Science – 1st: Is a butterfly a living or non-living thing? Give 2 reasons for how you know.	A butterfly is a living thing. Living things move and I see butterflies move. Butterflies grow too.	Living thing. It is not like a rock. It flies.
ELAR – 2nd Do you agree with the way Kimberly responded to her problem? Why?	Kimberly's problem was she got her library book wet. I disagree with the way Kimberly responded because she lied. When I lie, I get in lots more trouble. I think Kimberly should tell her teacher the truth.	No, she shouldn't lie. Lying is bad. Kimberly lied to her teacher.
Math – 3rd What is perimeter and how can you find the perimeter of an object?	Perimeter is the distance around the outside of something, like a fence. I can add up all of the sides of a shape to find perimeter.	For perimeter you add it all up. Like plus and plus another and plus another until you have it all. That's perimeter, you add it and add it until you have everything.
Social Studies - Kinder Why do people work? Give one example.	People work to help. My mom works at the gas station. She helps people get gas and cokes.	People work help. My mom gas station.

Content Area/ Assignment	Example	✗ Non-example
Science: Select 2 biomolecules and explain how the structure and function of each type of biomolecule helps support and sustain life.	Proteins and carbohydrates are both necessary in order for us to live. Proteins help give our cells their shape. The amino acids in proteins repair any damage, and they make cells stronger. Eating lots of proteins helps people who want to have big muscles that are defined. If we didn't eat proteins, our muscles would get really weak, and we wouldn't be able to support our own body. Proteins also help everything move around in our bodies and turn the foods we eat into stuff our bodies can use. Carbohydrates are also important but for different reasons. The sugars in carbohydrates give us short-term energy, which allows us to be productive each day. Having carbohydrates helps plants and animals with a hard shell keep their shape too. There are many different cells in the body, and carbohydrates help cells recognize each other so they can work together. As you can see, proteins and carbohydrates both have many functions that help our bodies work well.	Proteins are really important. Carbohydrates too. They are both biomolecules that help support and sustain life. The structure of proteins is what makes them so important and without eating proteins we can't live. We need carbohydrates too because they help our bodies. Lots of important functions that make them necessary. We couldn't do our jobs or exercise really good or anything without proteins and carbohydrates.

Content Area/ Assignment	Example	✖ Non-example
Social Studies: According to the 2009 census, there are approximately 38.5 million immigrants in the United States. The top four source countries of immigrants are: Mexico (30%), The Philippines (4.5%), India (4.3%), and China (3.7%). Pick one of the four source countries and answer the following question. Which two of the following categories do you think are significant considerations for people who immigrate to the United States from that country: political factors, economic factors, social factors, or environmental factors? Please support your answer with textual evidence.	In my opinion, the most significant consideration for people who immigrate to the United States from Mexico is economic factors. It all comes down to money, and many Mexicans do not make enough money to support their families. They are pulled to the US because there are more job opportunities here than in Mexico. American workers also earn higher salaries. Immigrating to a country like the US, with more available jobs and higher pay, would help Mexican immigrants make more money and get out of poverty. In addition to the economic factors, Mexicans also immigrate to the US for political reasons. There is a problem with drug cartels in Mexico, which makes their local governments unstable. The cartels try to influence and take over local governments and police officers. Mexicans immigrate because they feel unsafe where they live due to the high crime and violence from the cartels. Therefore, the most significant factors that pull Mexican immigrants to the United States are a stable and safe government (political) and more economic opportunity.	I think people that move here from Mexico do it for lots of reasons. More money. It's safer. Better schools. And there is not as many hurricanes that hit the United States either. When Hurricane Katrina hit us that was really bad, but if you live in Mexico they usually have many hurricanes like Hurricane Katrina that hit them all in one year. And even if they do not have a whole lot in one year, they might the next year. Hurricanes really like to head to that area of the world so that's why some people from there want to move to the United states. So they can be safe from hurricanes. Another reason is that lots of people in Mexico are really poor and so they want to move here to make more money. Lots more jobs in the US so they can make more money and not be poor anymore. I don't think Mexicans move here because of social factors. The rules are mostly the same in Mexico as they are in the US so they mainly move for money. They want to get a bigger paycheck for the work they do and most of the jobs here in the United States pay more than the same job in Mexico. So economic reasons are the biggest factor. And to get away from the violence and the hurricanes too.

Content Area/ Assignment	Example	✗ Non-example
Math: Jack and Jill are playing a game. There are six tiles in a box, 3 red and 3 blue. A player picks two tiles without looking. Jill gets a point if the tiles do not match; Jack gets a point if they do match. Explain why this is either a fair game or an unfair game.	I think this is an unfair game because the odds aren't even. Jack and Jill should have the same chance at getting a point, but they don't. There are 15 possible outcomes in the sample space. Only 6 of those would be two tiles that match. This means that the probability that Jack will get a point is 2/5. He has a 40% chance. The probability that Jill will get a point is 3/5, which is a 60% chance. In order for the game to be fair, both Jack and Jill should have an equally likely (50%) chance at getting a point.	Not a fair game. Jill would get more points and that's not fair. Jack is 2/5 and Jill is 3/5. If I were playing I would definitely want to be Jill. Tiles that don't match win. I'd try to play something else if I were Jack cuz he's gonna lose.
English Language Arts: Select one type of appeal that authors use to influence readers from this list: descriptions, anecdotes, case studies, analogies, illustrations. Explain how the technique can be used to influence the attitudes and actions of readers.	One type of appeal that authors use to influence readers is anecdotes. An anecdote is when an author tells a story to help convince the reader. The main reason anecdotes are effective is because they usually get the reader emotionally involved with the topic. For example, if an author wanted to convince the reader to enter the world of work right out of high school, instead of pursuing college, he/she might include an anecdote of a highly successful and happy person who went straight to the workforce. The author might even add another anecdote highlighting a specific college student's experience as miserable and depressing. Using anecdotes is a solid way to influence a reader because the story makes an emotional connection. Once a person's emotions are involved, he/she is more likely to act in response to those feelings.	Anecdotes is one appeal. Its when you tell a story to make your point. Like if I want to go straight to work after high school instead of going to college I could tell a story to convince my mom to let me do it. Like, "Mom, you know Mr. Mejia, he's been fixing our car since I was little. He started working at that shop right after he graduated high school and now look, he owns it and must make lots of money because he drives a nice ride and has a big house." So like if I told my mom that anecdote she might change her mind and go my way.

34. WHAT ARE THE TOP TWO FORMS OF ACADEMIC WRITING?

The top two forms of academic writing for students to master are: writing a clear explanation and making a claim with evidence. We see proof of this when looking at state standards for the core content areas. Clear explanations take different shapes in different disciplines. In math, it means identifying the steps in solving a mathematical problem. In science, it means describing cause and effect relationships. In social studies, it means explaining the factors that influenced historical events. In English language arts, it means analyzing the author's purpose.

Making a claim with evidence takes different shapes as well. In math, it means defending a solution to a word problem. In science, it means drawing a conclusion during an experiment. In social studies, it means arguing events in history from a certain perspective. In English language arts, it means persuading the reader of a certain point of view. State standards in all content areas require students to identify and analyze relationships, to describe and explain concepts, to consider various influences, and to analyze the impacts and results. Therefore, it makes sense to ask students to engage in those activities in writing.

35. What is a clear explanation?

Writing a clear explanation means teaching information to someone else on paper. The explanation needs to be concise, easy to understand, and it has to provide the reader with all the information needed to comprehend the topic. In the classroom, students are asked to write explanations of concepts/ideas like: What is homeostasis? At other times, they are asked to explain a process like: How do you solve this equation? All well-written explanations follow a similar format that we can explicitly teach to students.

1. Introduce the topic. State the purpose.
2. Provide information about the topic in the form of:
   - *Facts*
   - *Details*
   - *Examples/non-examples*
   - *Steps*
   - *Definitions/descriptions*
   - *Assumptions*
3. Restate the topic. State its significance.

There are countless graphic organizers and outlines that follow some variation of this format. On the surface it seems easy and even logical to follow this outline, but teachers consistently say that students have difficulty expanding or explaining their thinking. Students will write a brief response, one that is not fully developed. This is where explicit instruction becomes critical. I argue that students do not sufficiently develop their explanations because they are not sure what "add more details" or "explain this more" means.

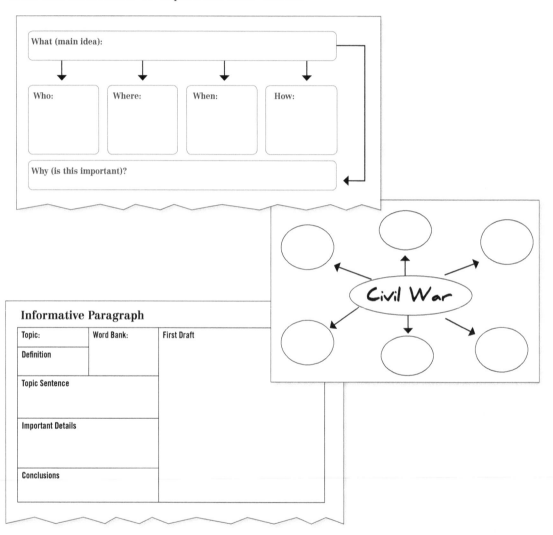

The body of a response, or the step where students provide information about the topic, is the area that needs clear definition, and many examples of information need to be included. The anchor chart that follows is an excellent teaching tool for developing a clear explanation. It can also serve as a resource for students who need support during future writing assignments.

Ways to Explain Your Thinking

Type	Description	Stem
Facts/ Details	Tell what you know.	I learned... I know that... One way to describe ____ is...
Examples	Give a specific person, idea, or thing.	One example is... _____ shows...
Steps 1. 2. 3. 4.	Tell ideas in order.	First... Next... Lastly...
Inferences	Tell your thinking.	I notice that... When I read ____, I think... This (*word, sentence, picture*) makes me think...

When introducing the anchor chart above, it is most effective to do so within the context of a current writing assignment. For example, if the class just finished an experiment in science, the teacher can use that context to teach students to focus on writing "steps" as highlighted in the chart. Teaching each of these ideas as an independent mini-lesson also supports younger students' ability to grasp the concept without getting overwhelmed. Primary teachers can create this chart together with their class over time.

Making a Clear Explanation: Ways to Expand and Explain Thinking

Type	Description	Question to ask myself
Facts	Provide true statements about the topic.	What would a Wikipedia entry about this topic say?
Details	Tell more about the topic. Answer: Who? What? When? Where? Why?	What information would the reader need to know about this topic? What is interesting about this topic? What else do I know about the topic?
Examples/ Non-example	Show what belongs within the topic and what belongs outside of the topic. Provide a sample that illustrates the topic.	Can I describe a situation that shows what I am trying to explain? What are specific examples of this topic?
Steps	Write information that tells what to do in a specific order.	What should the reader do next? Am I missing any steps?
Definitions/ Description	Tell what something means.	Do I need to explain any of the words in the writing?
Assumptions	Offer information about the topic that seems very basic and obvious.	What do I expect the reader to already know about the topic? What is the most basic information about this topic?

When introducing the anchor chart, it is important for teachers to model the way they use it. In doing so, students see how the process works before they try it on their own. Also, teachers can tell students there is another application for this chart. Students will be able to use it as a resource when offering feedback to writing partners.

> **Teacher:** Sometimes when I write, especially about new ideas, I have a hard time figuring out what to put on paper. It can be difficult to describe or explain an idea in detail so I've created an anchor chart to use as a resource. The chart lists many different ways to communicate my thinking in an expanded way. It is a great planning resource to use when beginning a writing task. When you begin, think about the writing task and determine which of the categories on the chart would best explain your thinking, just as I did. For example, you might decide that giving facts with an example and a non-example is the best approach for your writing. Or, the anchor chart can help if you reach a stuck point in your writing. Just take time to review all the questions in the right-hand column to know whether you are fully developing your topic. Another effective way to use this chart is to analyze your response when you finish writing. Then you can see any missed opportunities that can help expand your thoughts.

36. What does making a claim with evidence mean?

The goal of making a claim is to convince the reader to think the same way as the writer. This type of writing is called persuasive writing because it takes a position on an issue. In some cases, students are asked to argue one side of a complicated issue such as, "What is the most efficient way to solve this problem?" or "Do you agree or disagree that building the Great Wall of China was necessary?" An effective response to this type of question provides support for the side the writer chooses; it also addresses and refutes the arguments of the opposite side.

A claim does not always have opposing sides. In some instances students are asked to formulate an opinion about an academic concept such as, "Which constitutional amendment do you think has the most significant impact on American life?" Likewise, in an elementary classroom, a prompt might ask, "Which reading strategy helped you the most?" Students would need to support their claim but there aren't any counter-arguments. An effective response to this question would include evidence and reasoning to support the amendment the writer selected, but it does not necessarily need to include any counter-arguments. Regardless of the type of claim, in order to successfully persuade the reader, the claim must be well supported with evidence (facts) and reasoning (thinking that connects the facts with the claim). Just like a clear explanation, a well-written claim (persuasive response) will follow a predictable format that can be explicitly taught to students.

1. State the claim/position/argument.

2. Provide evidence to support the claim (or refute an opposing claim). Evidence includes:
   - Facts/Specific Details
   - Statistics
   - Examples
   - Expert Opinion/Authority
     Note: The text used in the Read section of each lesson will be the source of most or all of the evidence.

3. Provide reasoning to connect the evidence with the claim.*

4. Restate the claim. State its significance.

Repeat #2 and #3 as needed.

In addition to providing students with an outline for making a claim (or a graphic organizer that includes a similar structure), teachers must clearly explain, model, and give many examples of evidence and reasoning. Evidence is the information students pull from the text, and reasoning is the explanation they pull from their minds. They cannot write an effective persuasive response if they rely solely on the text or solely on their own thinking. Both text-based evidence and brain-based reasoning are necessary. Similarly, making a claim in written form is analogous to a courtroom trial. Imagine a defendant on trial for burglary. The prosecutor would provide as much physical evidence as possible (fingerprints at the crime scene, stolen items in the defendant's possession, etc.), but the evidence itself does not make the case. The prosecuting attorney must explain why the evidence is significant and link it directly back to the defendant. In persuasive writing, students must not only provide textual evidence, they must also act as the lawyer in a courtroom would act. They must explain why that particular evidence is significant, and they must link it directly to their claim.

In order to improve student ability to support claims with evidence, teachers must explicitly teach what "evidence" is. Teachers can use the next anchor chart to demystify the process of supporting a claim with evidence.

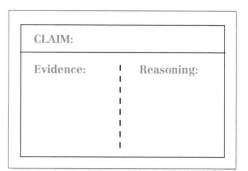

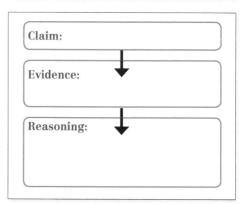

Using Evidence to Support Your Claim

Question: _____

Answer: _____
_____
_____

Supporting Evidence #1:_____

Where can can it be found in the text? _____

Supporting Evidence #2:_____

Making a Claim with Evidence: Ways to Expand and Explain Thinking

Type	Description	Questions to ask myself
Facts/Specific Details	Offer true statements about the claim. Give concrete information about the topic. Answer: Who? What? When? Where? Why?	What facts prove my thinking? What information will help to convince my audience that I am correct? What are the reasons for my claim? Why do I think my claim is right?
Statistics	Provide measurable, observable, quantifiable data related to the claim. Record numerical information about the claim.	Do I have any percentages, numbers, graphs, or other data that support my claim?
Examples	Illustrate the claim with a specific event, idea, person, etc.	What specific examples help me prove my claim? Has someone already made the same claim as I am making?
Expert Opinion/Authority	Provide statements or opinions from a source that has extensive knowledge of the topic.	What do the people who know the most about this topic have to say about the claim? Is there any previous research supporting the claim?

See the elementary version of this chart on p. 81

Example for introducing the anchor chart: Making a Claim with Evidence

Teacher: When you make a claim or try to convince the reader to agree with you, it is important to give evidence to support your claim. As the reader reads, he is probably thinking, "Why should I believe you? Why should I agree with you?" It is your job to give the reader as many reasons as possible. It is not enough to just make a claim. In fact, it is similar to times when your parents say, "No," and then when you ask, "Why not?" they say, "Because I said so."

"Because I said so" does not work in academic writing. We have to provide clear reasons for the reader to believe us. The "Ways to Expand and Explain Thinking" chart will help you think of different ways to build your argument. To persuade the reader, you will need to add facts/specific details, statistics, and examples. You will also need to give expert opinion/authority.

Even when students become skilled at identifying textual evidence, many struggle with applying reasoning to evidence. They have difficulty connecting and explaining how the fact, statistic, or example supports their claim. Students should be able to answer, "So what?" about each piece of evidence included in a response. One way to help students understand how to connect evidence with a claim is to provide them with concrete examples as well as non-examples. The following samples provide a starting point for explicitly teaching effective reasoning.

Claim: Economic push/pull factors are the most significant reason that Mexicans immigrate to the United States.	
❌ **Non-example:** Evidence without reasoning	Poverty is a common economic push factor. Many Mexicans live below the poverty line. The average income of a Mexican household is one quarter the average income of an American household.
✅ **Example:** Evidence with reasoning	Poverty is a common economic push factor. Many Mexicans live below the poverty line. Being able to get enough food to eat and enough money to live on is a struggle for many Mexicans, and they are always seeking ways to earn more money. Immigrating to a country like the U.S., a country with higher paying jobs, would help Mexican immigrants make more money and get out of poverty. The average income of a Mexican household is one quarter the average income of an American household. It makes sense then that Mexicans would want to move somewhere (the U.S.) that helps them potentially quadruple their income.

37. HOW DO I RESPOND WHEN STUDENTS ASK, "HOW LONG DOES IT NEED TO BE?"

It is often helpful to give students an estimated word count or number of sentences for an assignment, especially as they begin to write for academic purposes. Providing a range of between 300-400 words or between 2-4 sentences, for example, helps students plan and organize more effectively. It also prepares them for the writing tasks they will encounter beyond high school. Word counts are a common boundary set in college and professional writing tasks.

When determining an appropriate word count for an assignment, it is best for the teacher to actually complete the writing assignment and count the number of words in the response. This number will provide the basis for creating a flexible range of words for students. Completing the assignment ahead of time gives the teacher insight into possible obstacles students may encounter while writing. In addition, it provides a gauge for the amount of time the writing task will take. Both of these benefits positively inform lesson planning and delivery.

Overview of WRITE	Strategies
Clear Explanation	• Give students a clear purpose and audience for their written explanation. • Provide students with Ways to Expand and Explain Thinking chart. • Analyze examples and non-examples of written explanations.
Make a Claim with Evidence	• Give students a clear purpose and audience for their claims. • Provide students with Ways to Expand and Explain Thinking chart. • Analyze examples and non-examples of claims with evidence.

CAMPUS CONNECTIONS

1. What current opportunities to write do students have in class?

   _____

   _____

2. What, if any, adjustments should be made to our current writing practices?

   _____

   _____

3. What effect will example and non-example pieces have on our students?

   _____

   _____

Practice

1. Create a writing task for an upcoming unit of study.

   _____

   _____

2. With a partner, write 1-2 examples and non-examples of an upcoming writing task for students to analyze.

   _____

   _____

   _____

   _____

CHAPTER SIX
Gradual Release of Responsibility
and Other Considerations

*Scaffolding is support that
leads to independence.*
                    –John Seidlitz

38. WHAT IS THE GRADUAL RELEASE OF RESPONSIBILITY (GRR)?

It is important to get students to take responsibility for their learning, but it is even more important to have students buy into that idea. To make this happen in my classrooms, I talked to them about independent learning. I learned to give students responsibility for their learning, slowly. It had to be a gradual process for them and for me. After all, we all needed to be comfortable in the overall scheme of things. I knew I could not just let them go suddenly; I had to show them how to gain their independence. I still had to provide support sometimes, and during times when I was providing support, I would tell them, "Next time you'll be able to do more, or all, of this on your own." I'm sure it communicated my confidence in their ability to learn independently.

So how do teachers foster independence using the TRTW methodology? The answer to that question is quite logical. Teachers must gradually give the responsibility for talking, reading, and writing to the students. This gradual release of responsibility (GRR) is an educational practice that most teachers learn during their pre-service training (Pearson & Gallagher, 1983). By definition, it means to move students from dependence on the teacher to autonomy within each lesson. There are many ways that educational researchers communicate this idea, but essentially it is: "I do it, then we do it, then you do it."

Content area teachers naturally use the gradual release of responsibility when they plan lessons. This often takes the shape of direct teaching via lecture or mini-lesson, addressing questions or problems as a class, modeling examples and doing a task together as a group, and then giving students an individual task. In order for TRTW lessons to be consistently successful, teachers must imbed the GRR in each step of the process. That is, we cannot just tell students to talk, then read, then talk, then write. We must show them exactly how to do the talking, reading, and writing. We also need to do it with them before asking them to do it on their own.

Let's look at each step in the Gradual Release of Responsibility as it relates to a TRTW lesson.

"I do it" –

The teacher explains, shows, and models. The students observe.

During the "I do it" phase, the teacher provides direct instruction related to the task. Then the teacher models examples of each step in the TRTW process. She thinks aloud and actually completes the task in front of students so that they experience it as an observer. This is also an opportunity for the teacher to model a non-example in order to directly address any anticipated problems.

"We do it" –

The teacher prompts, responds, and scaffolds. The students try it out and practice.

This part of the GRR ensures that students practice talking, reading, and writing while still benefiting from the teacher's guidance. Think of this part as a student learning to ride a bike with training wheels. He is steering and pedaling, but he has support in case he starts to fall. In the "we do it" part of a lesson, the student talks, reads, and writes with his peers and his teacher. He is practicing academic communication, and he has the support of his teacher if he struggles. When teachers feel pressed for time, the "we do it" part of instruction usually gets shortened or removed. However, if students are to produce high-quality work, this is a vital part of the process. Just as no parent would expect a child to ride a bike after watching one demonstration, no teacher can reasonably expect a student to talk, read, and write on an academic level just by watching the teacher do it. Students must have multiple opportunities to practice alongside the "expert" in the classroom. Providing adequate "we do it" time eliminates the frustrating experience of assigning an independent task and then finding out that students are not ready/able to do it on their own.

K-5   *"You do it"* –

The teacher observes, evaluates, and assists as needed.
The students apply, problem solve, and practice.

The final part of the GRR is every teacher's ultimate goal, and the classroom looks like this: students engaging in academic conversations, comprehending academic texts, and producing academic responses...all by themselves. Ideally, students are prepared and successful while processing information and applying new learning on their own. During Talk #1 and Talk #2, as students work with their peers, their conversations are effective and productive.

It is noteworthy that this release process is dependent on the age, development, and abilities of your students. Younger students benefit from extended time in the "I do it" and "We do it" portions.

TALK #1	Description
I do it.	• The teacher responds to the conversation prompt aloud so students can hear what an appropriate response sounds like. • The teacher models a conversation with a student so other students can see and hear what the intended interaction looks and sounds like.
We do it.	• Students respond to the conversation prompt as the teacher provides specific feedback. • The teacher labels/names the thinking that students use when responding, encouraging high-quality responses, and offers suggestions for less effective responses.
You do it.	• Students engage in structured conversation with each other. • The teacher acts as facilitator among student partnerships/groups, framing and prompting as needed.

READ	Description
I do it.	• The teacher reads the text aloud and processes the information aloud as he/she reads. • The teacher thinks aloud using meta-cognitive strategies (see the Read section). Now, students can actually hear how meaning is created during reading.
We do it.	• The teacher continues to read a text aloud, and he/she processes the information aloud as he/she reads. • The teacher asks for students to share their thinking aloud. • Students think aloud while the teacher names and acknowledges student use of meta-cognitive strategies. • The teacher asks questions to drive student thoughts as they begin to read small chunks of text on their own.
You do it.	• Students read academic texts independently. • The teacher provides support on an individual basis, as needed.

TALK #2	Description
I do it.	• The teacher models several contributions he/she would make during a collaborative discussion of the text. • The teacher explains how his/her response was a high-quality contribution.
We do it.	• The teacher and students participate in a whole group discussion that mirrors the anticipated small group discussion. • The teacher conducts a fishbowl (a small discussion group) while the rest of the class observes. • The teacher and the observing students make comments about the conversation for the purpose of clarifying what small group discussions should sound like.
You do it.	• Students engage in structured conversation with each other. • The teacher acts as facilitator, framing and prompting among student groups, as needed.

WRITE	Description
I do it.	• The teacher writes a short answer response in front of the class. • The teacher makes his/her decisions transparent by thinking aloud while writing. • The teacher refers to the Ways to Expand and Explain Thinking anchor charts and uses them while thinking aloud and while writing.
We do it.	• The students and the teacher co-write a short answer response. • The teacher asks guiding questions as they coauthor the response to be sure the student input is on target. • The teacher shares a non-example with students. Then he/she asks students to analyze why the sample is considered poor quality. Together, the teacher and the students revise it.
You do it.	• Students write an academic response independently. • The teacher provides support on an individual basis, as needed.

39. WHAT ABOUT SPECIAL POPULATIONS?

Today's classrooms have all types of learners. Some require special consideration because they bring a unique set of needs to the classroom. This section is not intended to provide an extensive treatment of special populations of students, but rather to give some general guidelines and ways to support these students.

40. How can I accommodate English learners?

English learners are trying to understand challenging content area concepts while simultaneously trying to learn the English language. This is a very daunting task indeed. Imagine trying to learn or master something difficult, like how to implant an artificial intraocular lens. Imagine having to listen to instruction and read informational text in a different language about the topic, say, Swahili. (If you happen to be fluent in Swahili, substitute a language you do not know how to speak.) In order to be successful, you would most definitely need extra support, but as you become more proficient with both the topic and the new language, you would need less and less support. The same is true for English learners.

Teachers must take into account an English learner's limited ability to use academic English, and teachers need to make instructional adjustments based on that information. The resulting changes are called linguistic accommodations. A good way to begin thinking about imbedding appropriate linguistic accommodations in a TRTW lesson is to think personally about being a learner in the above scenario. Ask yourself, "What would I need in order to be able to listen to, talk, read, and write about cataract surgery in Swahili?"

An answer to that question brings some basic linguistic accommodations to mind. The next three supports represent some of the most fundamental and effective pathways to help English learners find success in a TRTW lesson.

Non-Linguistic Representation

First, lots of pictures are needed. Visual support is critical for students who are not proficient in English. In fact, providing non-linguistic representations throughout the TRTW lesson is vital for the English learner to understand content. Pictures are not the only avenues, however. Non-linguistic support can take many forms—photographs, drawings, gestures, role-plays, physical models, mental pictures, graphic organizers, movement activities, manipulatives, and the use of real objects. The goal is to give students access to the content in a way that is not bound by the English language. Intentionally making non-linguistic representation a regular component in lessons will help level the playing field for students who are not yet proficient in English. It is important that teachers consistently refer to the visuals during instruction by pointing and gesturing to charts, posters, or graphs in the classroom.

Sentence Stems (also called sentence starters or frames)

Another powerful linguistic accommodation is the sentence stem; it guides oral and written communication. Giving students a sentence beginning for a response eliminates the blank page effect. Think back to the reports and papers assigned in college or graduate school. When all the reading and research was complete and it was time to write, the blank screen of the computer seemed to just sit there and stare. Some folks would get up to make a cup of coffee and then try again, get up to fold the laundry and then try again, get up to get the mail and then try again. The process of battling the blank screen could go on for hours. And so it is with English learners. Not only do they experience the same phenomena in writing, but it happens in oral exchanges as well. While they may have a significant understanding of content, they are unsure about communicating their thoughts in English. The sentence stem kick-starts their ability to communicate and gives them the linguistic momentum that helps them participate.

A second significant benefit of using sentence stems in content area classrooms is to guarantee the use of academic language by students. When students use the stem as part of their oral or written responses, they get deliberate exposure to the academic terminology with which they struggle. For example, during the Talk #1 section of a social studies lesson, the teacher might ask students to discuss the characteristics of a totalitarian government. Without the stem, the English learner may not say anything, or say something like, "The state runs everything," or "No choice for the people." If, however, the teacher linguistically accommodates the interaction by providing a sentence stem such as, "One characteristic of a totalitarian government is...," the English learner's response would sound like this: "One characteristic of a totalitarian government is that the state runs everything." Using the stem for support, students are able to use academic vocabulary in a response.

Additionally, stems support English learners' ability to speak in a complete sentence. Imagine an elementary lesson on shapes. During Talk #2, the teacher gives partnerships a triangle and square and asks them to describe how they are alike and different. Without any stems, students might point and say, "Square 4. This 3." With stems like, "A _____ has ____ sides," or "Triangles and squares are different because...," students begin to internalize complete thoughts.

Adapted Text

Because the TRTW lesson is anchored by an academic text that each student must read, it is important to analyze the text through the eyes of an English learner. Can they read the text as it is written? In what way/s is this text too difficult for English learners to read and understand? The challenge is to adapt the text to make it accessible to students with limited English proficiency. An adapted text is an altered form of the original text that reduces the readability demands. It reduces long, complicated sentences into simpler sentences, and it adds definitions for specialized terminology. In addition, it keeps the major academic concepts intact (Echevarria, Vogt, & Short, 2008). While adapting text, the integrity of the academic concepts must be maintained. If the text is oversimplified, the content can be diminished or lost altogether. Note: Often, textbook companies include an adapted text or native language resource, either online or in the ancillary materials.

Example of Original Text:
Spain's concessions to the rebels enraged many Spanish loyalists in Cuba. In January 1898, the loyalists rioted in Havana. Worried that American citizens in Cuba might be attacked, McKinley made the fateful decision to send the battleship Maine to Havana in case the Americans had to be evacuated (Appleby et al., 2003).

Example of Adapted Text for Students with Beginning Proficiency in English:
Spain had to give many things to the rebels. This made many Spanish loyalists (people in Cuba who supported Spain) angry. The loyalists rioted (yelled and fought in the streets) in the city of Havana. President McKinley thought Americans might be attacked in Cuba. He decided to send a battleship called the Maine to Havana. The ship would help people escape.

Example of Adapted Text for Students with Advanced Proficiency in English:
Many people in Cuba who supported Spain (Spanish loyalists) were very angry when Spain gave the rebels what they wanted. In January of 1898, the angry loyalists began rioting (yelling and fighting) in the city of Havana. President McKinley was worried that the loyalists might attack the American citizens who lived in Cuba. He decided to send a battleship named Maine to Havana. If the loyalists attacked the Americans, then the Americans could evacuate (leave the city) and get on the battleship. President McKinley's decision to send the battleship to Havana is a very important one.

Adapting a text can be a time-consuming undertaking, but for students who find the original text too difficult, it is the most effective accommodation. I recommend that teachers take the "divide and conquer" approach to adapting text. If there are three U.S. History teachers on campus, for example, then each can rotate adapting the anchor text for the next topic of study. Then they all get three adapted texts for the time it takes to adapt just one. Teachers can also utilize campus or district ESL specialists or content area coaches to help them with this task as well. Often these specialized teachers have access to resources for, and training in, adapted texts.

There are several alternatives to adapting the text itself. Teachers can support English learners' comprehension by providing a version of the text that has simple notes recorded in the margin or with key sentences or phrases that are highlighted. Giving students a graphic organizer that visually clarifies the purpose for reading and/or a teacher-prepared outline can also help English learners hone in on the most important ideas in the text (Echevarria, Vogt, & Short, 2008). Those students who are just beginning to learn English may also benefit from having access to the text—or at least information about the academic concept—in their native language.

OTHER LINGUISTIC ACCOMMODATIONS FOR ENGLISH LEARNERS

By its very nature, the TRTW format provides linguistically accommodated access to the content. When teachers change the delivery of content from "direct teach then assignment" to "talk, read, talk, write," they are giving English learners increased exposure to academic English in all four language domains. Depending on their level of proficiency in English, however, students may need additional support. The chart that follows will guide your instructional decisions and ensure that English learners are successful during a TRTW lesson.

When working with English learners, it is important to determine the type of support to offer. The goal is to set the stage so the English learner will not only be successful, but independently successful in the future.

Linguistic Accommodations by Language Domain*		
Listening/Speaking Supports for English learners during Talk #1 and Talk #2	**Reading** Supports for English learners during the Read section	**Writing** Supports for English learners during the Write section
• Teach phrases so students can request others to repeat, slow down, or rephrase. • Allow extra thinking and rehearsal time before expecting an oral response. • Model pronunciation and use choral response. • Give students multiple opportunities to speak in varied contexts. • Use native language support, including same language peers to clarify concepts. • Use peer interaction.	• Organize reading into meaningful "chunks" of text. • Allow students to demonstrate comprehension through drawing and/or native language, as needed. • Use peer collaboration. • Scan for unknown terms before reading and pre-teach those terms. • Use text for multiple purposes. • Provide graphic organizers or guided questions.	• Provide completed samples. • Give examples and non-examples of expected outcomes. • Use genre analysis to identify and use features of English writing. • Provide concrete feedback for student writing. • Model thinking aloud when writing. • Create multiple opportunities for students to write using newly acquired vocabulary.

Adapted from ELPS Flip Book *(Seidlitz, 2010)*

41. How can I accommodate students with a reading disability?

Students with a reading disability can have a wide range of challenges when interacting with academic texts. Reading disabilities range from phonological deficits (hearing sounds) and decoding, to fluency and naming, to impaired ability to comprehend. When working with a student with a reading disability, it is imperative to use that student's Individual Education Plan (IEP) as a roadmap. Depending on the nature of that student's disability, some of the accommodations mentioned in the section above may also be part of his IEP.

In general, the gradual release of responsibility for this group of students is significantly more gradual than the general student population. It makes sense that students who struggle with reading will need more time observing good models ("I do it.") and reading in the company of more skilled readers ("We do it.") before moving toward independent reading. To determine realistic goals and expectations, refer to each student's IEP and consult with the special education team on your campus.

CAMPUS CONNECTIONS

1. What are the benefits of teaching and talking about meta-cognition with your struggling learners?

2. In which step of the Gradual Release of Responsibility (I do it, We do it, or You do it) are you anticipating the most difficulty?

3. What would a Gradual Release of Responsibility look like in your classroom?

4. Which accommodations for English learners have you tried in the past? What were the results?

5. What successes have you had in meeting the needs of struggling students?

Practice

1. With a partner, practice the "I do" sections in the Gradual Release of Responsibility with an upcoming unit of study. Pay particular attention to "thinking aloud" while speaking. (See charts on pp. 91-93 for reference.)

2. Identify all of your students who may need special consideration during a TRTW lesson. (These students include any who have a disability, limited English language proficiency, or any other learning difference.)

CHAPTER SEVEN
Questions from the Field

*To raise new questions, new possibilities,
to regard old problems from a new angle,
requires creative imagination and marks
real advance in science.*

–Albert Einstein

42. HOW DO I PLAN A TRTW LESSON?

While teachers have different approaches to planning, the steps below consistently result in high-quality TRTW lessons:

1. Standard: Determine the standard for the lesson (CCSS, TEKS, etc.)
The goal of a TRTW formatted lesson is the same as the goal for any other lesson: to teach a standard. Therefore, is it important to begin the planning process with the standard.

2. Read: Find or create a text that provides the necessary content for that standard. Remember the text is replacing the teacher's direct teaching of the content. The text itself will be the main source of information about the standard. Identify a clear purpose for students to read the text by asking yourself, "What specifically do I want students to learn from reading this?"

3. Write: Create a writing task that will effectively demonstrate students' levels of understanding of the content they read. The writing assignment should be directly linked to the standard itself. This is both the student's and the teacher's primary avenue for assessing learning.

4. Talk #2: Generate talking tasks that will help students gain deeper insights into the text, clarify understanding of the content, clear up any confusions, and provide time for continued processing of information.

5. Talk #1: Design a talking task that will bring students into the lesson.

6. Additional supports: Think about which students may need additional supports throughout the lesson. Prepare any accommodations or modifications at this time. It is also a good idea to create a plan for how you, the teacher, will spend your time during each component of the lesson. For example, while students are reading the text, you might plan to work with an individual student, or pull a small group.

43. HOW DO I ASSESS LEARNING IN A TRTW LESSON?

There are many ways to assess student learning within the confines of a TRTW lesson. Students' written output during the Write section of the lesson could be used as a summative assessment. Teachers can grade those paragraphs based on the task assigned. Teachers can also create an assignment for students to complete after the lesson to demonstrate understanding. Aside from these two options for grading, there are innumerable opportunities for teachers to collect formative assessment data. While students are reading, teachers can read and monitor student notes to gauge their understanding. Conferencing with students as they read and write will give the teacher the most accurate means for assessing learning. Additionally during Talk #2, it is critical for teachers to facilitate group conversations to determine how well and deeply students are processing the new information. Many teachers use a rubric or checklist during Talk #2 to evaluate student participation. Another common way teachers gain formative assessment data is by asking students to self reflect and provide feedback on their peers after Talk #2 is over. Below are some sample checklists and rubrics for informally assessing Talk #2.

STUDENT NAME	Interacts with respect	Builds on ideas of others	Uses the text to support thinking	Makes connections	Communicates thinking clearly	Actively listens to others	Asks questions that deepen the discussion
Mariah							
Johnny							
Carlos							
Hiroki							
Deon							
Jessi							
Kelsey							
Whitney							
Abdul							
Shanna							
Jared							
Chandell							
Mary							
Lucy							
Travis							
Darius							
Jordan							
Taylor							
Nima							
Elsa							
Arthur							
Roberto							

CATEGORY	4	3	2	1
Participation	Student actively contributes relevant and insightful comments, and poses thoughtful questions.	Student willingly participates in classroom discussions.	Student responds to prompts but seldom volunteers. Comments are sometimes off topic.	Student rarely participates and never volunteers. Comments are seldomly relevant.
Comprehension	Student comments reflect a deep understanding.	Student comments indicate good understanding.	Student comments indicate some understanding, with gaps or some confusion.	Student comments indicate little to no understanding.
Respect for Others	Student actively listens, waits patiently, and is respectful of other points of view.	Student listens to others, rarely interrupts, and generally accepts other points of view.	Student does not consistently listen to others, interrupts frequently and demonstrates little respect for other points of view.	Student typically does not listen to others, interrupts frequently and/or is rude and intolerant of other points of view.

Team Member	Did not participate appropriately 😢	Participation was appropriate 🙂	Participation was exceptional 😄

44. WHEN SHOULD I USE THE TRTW APPROACH?

The TRTW approach can be used in a variety of ways.

Teachers can use TRTW as:

An **introductory lesson** to a topic or unit of study for the purposes of building background.
For an example, see p.124: 3rd grade Simile lesson.

A **follow-up lesson** on a previously taught topic (think day two or three of a unit) for the purpose of extended learning and applying concepts.
For an example, see p.122: 2nd grade Character Response lesson.

A **summative lesson** for the purpose of synthesizing learning over multiple lessons.
For an example, see p.149: High School World Geography Migration, Push/Pull Factors.

A **vocabulary lesson** for the purpose of defining and explaining new terminology.
For an example see p.148: Exterior/Interior Angles.

45. My students don't listen to each other.
HOW CAN I INCREASE LISTENER ACCOUNTABILITY?

Being a good listener is a lifelong skill. Even adults often struggle with truly engaging with what others are saying to them. If conversation is to be successful, we must think of listening as a process we must teach. We cannot just tell students to listen to each other; rather, we must teach what that looks like and sounds like as well as build in supports and expectations for it to occur. For example, active listening looks like: *Eyes on the speaker, and body facing the speaker.*

Here are some teachable routines that hold students accountable for active listening. They can be used in isolation or in combination:

Quick jot – As group members are talking, each member is responsible for recording a "quick jot" (word or phrase that will help them remember what the speaker shared).

Retell then Add – Before a student shares his/her thinking, he/she must paraphrase what the previous speaker said first and then can add his/her thinking.

Random selection – As the teacher monitors and facilitates the conversations, he/she randomly selects a group member to share the content of what was discussed before he/she arrived. Teachers should explicitly communicate that he/she will be randomly selecting students before discussions begin so that students can be prepared.

MVC – Ask each member to listen carefully to their peers because at the end of the dialogue they must select the Most Valuable Contribution (MVC) to the discussion. They cannot select their own contribution.

Follow-up question – Ask each member to listen closely to each speaker so that they can ask a follow-up question to that speaker when they are finished. This slows down the dialogue enough for each person to fully engage with each speaker.

46. IS IT OK IF I CHANGE THE ORDER OF THE TRTW TASKS?

When I work with teachers to implement TRTW in their classroom and they begin a question with, "Is it ok if…" my response is generally yes. Many of those questions stem from the order of this process. Questions like:

• Do I always have to do both Talk #1 and Talk #2?
• My students need to jot down their ideas before they talk to their partners during Talk #1. Is that ok?
• Can I have them talk a third time after they finish their written response?
• What if they read and then write and do Talk #2 at the end?

It is so important to plan lessons with your specific students' needs and abilities in mind. Many classes can work through a TRTW lesson as defined in the earlier chapters in this book, but there are certainly other classroom situations that could require an adapted approach. For example, some teachers have students write their response to Talk #1 during the first 2 minutes of class because they know that after socializing in the hall during class change, students need a quiet way to get settled into the lesson. Another common variation, especially in classrooms with English learners, is to ask students to read their written paragraph to 1-2 other students at the end of each lesson in order to increase their oral language practice.

The order of the literacy tasks isn't nearly as important as the tasks themselves. If students are reading, writing, and talking about the content, they are growing in disciplinary knowledge while acquiring lifelong literacy skills.

47. HOW CAN I DIFFERENTIATE DURING A TRTW LESSON?

There are many ways to differentiate within this approach. The text itself is a differentiation point. For example, a teacher can provide a grade level article to the majority of the students in his/her class and a simplified version of the same article to any readers who are not proficient enough to read the original text. The same teacher could offer a more advanced option as well, possibly offering those students a bank of resources to read in order to meet the same purpose for reading. Other ways to differentiate the text include providing copies with key points highlighted, giving teacher notes in the margin of the text, online versions of the text, and/or native language text.

Differentiating the task is another effective option. For example, a teacher can select more than one purpose for reading a text. Some students might read to identify literal or basic information, while others might read to evaluate the author's message. If using a Pay Attention To List (see p. 43), the teacher can provide more than one version in order to specifically target what individual students should focus on during the reading. The Write task does not need to be the same for all students, either.

Students might need differentiation within the talking tasks as well. Teachers can give sentence stems and word banks to students who might need them. Another option is to provide different questions to different groups of students. Some discussion groups might need one question at a time, others could benefit from a list of questions that increase in complexity, while others can randomly pick questions to discuss in any order.

Lastly, the structure of this approach "frees up" the teacher's time. While students are talking, reading, and writing, the teacher can determine who needs individualized support and provide it.

48. HOW CAN I IMPLEMENT TRTW IN AN ELEMENTARY CLASSROOM?

TRTW is a practical approach and can be used in all grade levels. Students in Kindergarten through 5th grade can benefit from using this literacy-based routine just like students in upper grades. It is important to note that the TRTW approach should not replace your current reading program. Teachers should continue to use research-based reading practices such as guided reading, balanced literacy, reader's workshop, etc. to teach students basic reading skills. TRTW, however, emphasizes the process of reading to learn. It will provide students the opportunity to practice the basic reading skills and use them across the curriculum. It can be routinely used during math, science, social studies, art, music, and in any other content area.

For elementary students, who are still developing their abilities to decode and comprehend text independently, TRTW might look a little different. Depending on your students' literacy skills, various components of this approach might need additional scaffolds. The chart on the next page provides options for what each TRTW component may look like. They range from "highly supported" to "highly independent."

TALK #1	READ	TALK #2	WRITE
• Teacher modeling • Choral Response of an individual student's idea *(example below)* • Teacher brainstorms possible responses with the whole class, records them on chart paper, and then asks students to use one of those with their partner *(example below)* • Sentence stems	• Teacher modeling • Text on tape • Partner reading • Teacher reads, students repeat • Reread familiar text	• Teacher modeling • Strategic number of members in each group • Create talking routines with sentence stems • Use props	• Teacher Modeling • Drawing • Labeling • Students dictate ideas while teacher records them • Completing sentence stems

Choral Response of an individual student's idea

Rather than partners or student groups talking to each other, the teacher maintains a whole class discussion. After one student is called upon, the teacher repeats what that student shared and then asks the entire class to repeat it.

For example:

Teacher: How do you know if a shape is 2 dimensional?
Students raise their hands and the teacher calls on Wynona.

Wynona: It's flat.

Teacher: Great. 2 Dimensional shapes are flat. Let's all repeat: "2 Dimensional shapes are flat."

Whole Class: 2 Dimensional shapes are flat.

Teacher: What is another way we can tell that a shape is 2 dimensional? Yes, Ricardo?

Teacher brainstorms possible responses with the whole class, records them (on chart paper, document camera, smart board, dry erase board, etc.) and then asks students to use one of those with their partner

For example:

Teacher to the whole class: "What are some forms of transportation? How can you get from one place to another?"

Teacher calls on 5 students and records their responses on a class chart.

Teacher: Let's read our list together.
(Together with class)
"Walk, Airplane, Bike, Car, Scooter."
Now I want you to turn to your partner and tell them 2 forms of transportation.

> **Modes of Transportation**
>
> Walk
>
> Airplane
>
> Bike
>
> Car
>
> Scooter

49. WHAT ABOUT NEWCOMERS?

Newcomers are students who have recently immigrated and are at the very beginning stages of learning English. The TRTW approach centers on students reading, writing, and speaking in English, all skills that most newcomers do not yet possess. Therefore, teachers of newcomers will need to identify each student's language proficiency levels using the proficiency level descriptors (PLDs) to determine appropriate levels of participation and output. Newcomers may be in their silent period, which is a short space of time when the beginners are not comfortable speaking because they've not yet grown accustomed to the sounds and rhythms of the new language. If this is the case, allowing for some nonparticipation can be an appropriate accommodation.

Many newcomers have a strong desire to acquire oral language skills. They want to be able to communicate socially, and they know that they need academic language as well. Teachers can capitalize on this by structuring Talk #1 and Talk #2 with the newcomer in mind. Some ways to do this include: explicitly teaching the use of cognates; intentionally using clear diction, intonation, and expression while speaking in English; encouraging them to practice and repeat what other group members say; and providing them with simple stems for responding. Newcomers benefit from being part of a group, even if their participation is primarily as an observer. In order to increase their comprehension of the conversation and knowledge of the content being discussed, the teacher should include other sheltered strategies such as visuals, slower rate of speech, repetition, and "point and talk" when facilitating the discussion groups. If there is a native language peer, encourage newcomers to engage in the talking tasks using their native language. When students have opportunities to use their first language, certain comprehension strategies are accessed and students are able to make connections to the topic being discussed (Pacheco, David, & Jimenez, 2015). This helps students begin to participate rather than "opting out" due to fears about their English proficiency.

During the Read portion of a TRTW lesson, newcomers require significant support. If they have reading proficiency in their native language, it can be effective to provide a native language version of the text, a highly adapted version that is written in simple, present tense English, or oral clarification of the text in the native language. Offering opportunities for newcomers to track print while someone reads a section (or key parts of a section) aloud is another great scaffold. Tracking print is simply following words from left to right and top to bottom with your finger. Doing this while the teacher or a peer reads aloud is brain-friendly, builds English sight words and allows the newcomer to participate in the Read part meaningfully, while simultaneously addressing proficiency level needs. As with the Talk and Write sections of the lesson, it is critical that teachers use each student's emerging proficiency levels in English (based on the PLDs) to determine reasonable expectations.

TRTW lessons end with students demonstrating their learning through writing. Encouraging newcomers to write in their native language helps them to solidify and reflect on their learning while still engaging in the writing process. Providing newcomers an alternative way to demonstrate learning (drawing, orally explaining in native language, labeling/listing, sorting visuals, showing/role playing, etc.) also supports the lesson outcome while taking into consideration their beginning/intermediate proficiency levels in English.

Another goal for newcomers during the Write section is to improve their ability to write in English. This might include translating some of their native language writing, completing simple sentence frames, or recording an oral explanation on paper with adequate support.

Finally, the Read and Write sections are an ideal opportunity for teachers to provide individualized support to newcomers. Teachers can use this time, while the rest of the class is reading and writing independently, to further develop newcomers' content knowledge and English proficiency through one-on-one or small group interactions. Newcomers need focused, targeted, and systematic second language instruction, and now teachers have the time to provide it during the Read and Write sections.

50. HOW DOES TRTW LOOK IN A PULL OUT/RESOURCE/INTERVENTION CLASS?

There are two considerations for pull out/resource/intervention type classes: class size and each student's ability level. Most pull out/resource/intervention classes are small, usually ranging from 3-10 students. This becomes a factor when thinking about the Talk portions of the lesson. Instead of having students partner up or split into groups like a teacher would in a general education setting, in this setting, the Talk portions can remain "whole group." For example, if a teacher has only 5 students in the class, he can offer the discussion topic or question and then facilitate the group conversation. Students in these classes need extra support; therefore, it is ideal for the teacher to remain part of the discussion, providing constant scaffolds to ensure students are successful.

The Read and Write portions may need to be "shared" with the teacher rather than independent tasks, based on the abilities of the students in the class. Selecting a text that is appropriate for the reading level of the students is another important consideration. When making your selection of text and grouping configurations, review relevant student data (i.e., Individual Education Plans (IEPs), Proficiency Level Descriptors (PLDs), benchmarks, reading level, state assessment data, etc.) to make purposeful decisions.

51. DO TRTW LESSONS HAVE TO LAST THE ENTIRE CLASS PERIOD?

Of course not! The approach is highly adaptable for any amount of time, ranging from 5 minutes to several class periods. A collapsed version could be as simple as asking students to do a quick "turn and talk" for 1 minute (Talk #1), then asking them to read something short (i.e., a slide projected on the Smartboard, paragraph of a book, word problem) for 1-3 minutes (Read), then giving them a chance to explain or summarize what they read to their partner for 1 minute (Talk #2), and finally asking them to jot down their thinking/learning in their journal for 1-2 minutes (Write). Teachers can also expand TRTW to include a much longer text, more substantial writing assignment, and provide extended dialogue time as appropriate for any given topic in the curriculum.

52. HOW OFTEN SHOULD I USE THE TRTW APPROACH?

It is helpful to think of the TRTW approach as a classroom routine, or a habit for learning. In order to form this habit, there must be repetition and consistency. Initially, it is valuable to use this approach often; otherwise, teachers end up spending precious class time reteaching the routine, rather than using the routine to teach content.

In elementary classrooms, a teacher who teaches many subjects may use it multiple times throughout the school day. A self-contained 2nd grade teacher might use TRTW in math for a word problem and in science for an article, as well as use it with a specific small group during reading time.

In secondary classrooms, teachers often use TRTW as a regular routine within a larger unit. For example, an 8th grade history teacher might consistently use it as a 2nd day lesson once he has introduced a topic on the first day. In this scenario students would engage using TRTW once per unit, whether the unit is 3 lessons long or 8 lessons long.

Based on the feedback from teachers who are successful with TRTW, a general guideline for implementation is 1-3 times per week per subject.

53. HOW LONG DOES IT TAKE TO PLAN A TRTW LESSON?

Like any new approach, planning your first few TRTW lessons can be time consuming, and may take several hours. Finding an appropriate text for students to read that is aligned to the standard is often the biggest hurdle for teachers to overcome. Another aspect of planning that takes time is crafting discussion questions for Talk #2 that are powerful. It is often hard to break away from asking questions that have one right answer to move toward truly thought-provoking and open-ended questions. The more lessons you plan, the more efficient you will become. With practice, many teachers can plan TRTW lessons in 20-30 minutes. Teachers who plan as a team are often able to craft TRTW lessons very quickly because there are many ideas for texts, and many ideas for discussion questions. If planning a lesson in this format is a struggle, it is helpful to ask for help from your campus and district specialists as well as any peers who are also implementing TRTW.

54. I DO NOT TEACH A CORE SUBJECT. WILL TRTW WORK FOR ME?

Yes! Teachers of all subjects are using TRTW, including foreign language, AVID, English as a Second Language, CTE, and electives teachers. Most courses lend themselves well to asking students to talk, read, and write about the content they are learning. Even in classes where all 4 components might not be applicable, teachers can modify the approach to suit their needs. For example, a PE coach who is teaching a new skill on the field can begin with a Talk #1 question for partners to discuss (Talk #1). Rather than giving them a text and purpose for reading, which wouldn't make sense on the field, he/she can tell them the purpose for watching his/her demonstration of the skill. They can watch and practice the skill, in lieu of reading (Read). Following repeated practice, the PE coach can then ask partners to discuss the technique and what they learned as they practiced (Talk #2). In most PE scenarios like the one described here, the Write section might not be possible due to time and logistics. The benefits of structured talk before and after the demonstration, as well as the teacher clearly stating a purpose for watching the demonstration, fully support the goals of TRTW, increased student engagement, and will undoubtedly improve their comprehension of the learning goal (the new skill on the field).

55. HOW CAN INTERVENTIONISTS, COACHES, AND SUPPORT STAFF REINFORCE THE CLASSROOM TEACHER'S IMPLEMENTATION?

There are many ways for support staff members to help. Some ideas include:
- Model a lesson using the TRTW approach while teachers observe.
- Observe teachers implementing TRTW and provide feedback.
- Co-teach TRTW lessons, allowing for two adults to facilitate students reading, writing, and talking.
- Plan TRTW lessons with teachers.
- Find or write appropriate texts for teachers to use.
- Generate a bank of open-ended question stems for teachers to use during Talk #2.
- Lead groups of teachers in peer observations of TRTW lessons so teachers can learn from each other.

56. CAN I USE THIS APPROACH WITH MULTIPLE TEXTS?

Yes, using multiple texts can work within the TRTW design. For example, an English class might be examining how an author's word choice impacts the mood of a story. The teacher might have 4 different texts that are good examples of an author's word choice. She can give 5 students the first text, 5 students the second text, and so on. The entire class is reading for the same purpose, but the text is different. During Talk #2, the teacher can strategically put students who read different material in the same group to explain how word choice impacted their specific text.

57. WHAT SHOULD I THINK ABOUT WHEN EVALUATING WHETHER A TEXT IS APPROPRIATE FOR A CLASS?

Some considerations for selecting a text include:

- Content: Is the content tightly aligned with the standard being taught? Will comprehending the text result in meeting the learning goal?

- Ability: Can my students read it? Is this text too difficult for my students to independently comprehend? Do I need to provide alternatives for some of my students?

- Time: Will students be able to read this in the allotted amount of time? Should I ask them to only read a specific section of the text?

If your existing curriculum materials and your search for material on your own do not produce texts that meet the criteria above, write the text yourself. You know your content and the students you teach, so the text you produce will inevitably be the most effective.

58. In my class, some students read faster than others.
HOW DO I HANDLE EARLY FINISHERS AND THOSE WHO CANNOT COMPLETE THE READING IN THE ALLOTTED AMOUNT OF TIME?

The fact that students have varied rates of reading is a constant challenge in a TRTW lesson. Some supports for students who read more slowly include:

- Provide pre-exposure to the text (i.e., sharing in a small group before the lesson, giving it to students to read for homework the night before, allowing any support teacher who works with the student to use the same text with them).

- Provide a shortened version of the text.

- Provide a highlighted version of the text, or direct students to the section of text that is most critical for the lesson.

- Allow for some partner reading.

- Work one-on-one or in a small group with these students during the Read time.

Some options for students who complete the reading more quickly (early finishers) include:
- Allow them to read self-selected text.
- Challenge them to generate 1-3 possible discussion questions for Talk #2.
- Allow students to engage in any pre-existing "early finisher" tasks you have available within your classroom.
- Collaborate with students to find a mutually agreeable task for the extra time.

All students, no matter their rate of reading, benefit when the teacher gives them a clear expectation for the amount of time allotted for the reading task. It is also helpful to provide a few additional time cues such as: "We're about halfway through our reading time." Or, "Try to finish the section you are reading now. We'll stop reading time in 1 minute."

59. HOW DO YOU DETERMINE HOW MUCH TIME TO GIVE STUDENTS TO TALK DURING TALK #2?

Unfortunately, there is not a magic number of minutes that will result in effective conversation. We need to consider how skilled our students are at academic conversations, the quantity of topics to be discussed, and the amount of time available. In general, a student conversation for Talk #2 is between 3-10 minutes, but very few classes begin with that amount of time. During initial TRTW lessons, 1-2 minutes may be appropriate and then as students become more proficient with academic dialogue, the amount of time for talk can increase.

The best way to answer the "time" question is to observe your students while they are talking. When groups stop talking, get off task, or start repeating themselves, those can be signals that you have given them too much time to talk. As you facilitate conversations it is important to consistently scan the room to gauge the conversations. Once you see 1-2 groups finishing or getting off task, give a 30 second warning and then end Talk #2.

Another approach to the "time" question is to ask your students to signal when they've had enough time. Some teachers use a signal, like raise your hand, or a physical object, like placing a plastic cup or index card in a specific location. When the teacher sees the signal as he/she is scanning the room, he/she can go directly to that group to extend the conversation, or if several groups are signaling, bring Talk #2 to a close. One benefit to this is that we are returning responsibility back to our students.

60. WHAT DO I DO DURING THE TALK TIME?

The teacher's primary role while students are talking is to actively facilitate those conversations by moving about the room, checking in with groups, prompting with additional questions, and providing thoughtful feedback to student responses. As student groups become skilled at conversation, teachers may also choose to use this time to lead a small group or work individually with a student.

Other effective ways for the teacher to show support during the Talk times include:
- collecting formative assessment data by noting individual student responses;

- providing positive reinforcement of desired behaviors and skills (either individually, at a group, or to the whole class);

- targeting specific students to observe and support (ex: newcomers, shy students, students who "take over" discussions, struggling learners, etc.).

CAMPUS CONNECTIONS

Discuss

1. Which question and answer is most significant for you?

2. How often should you be conducting TRTW lessons given your grade and subject?

3. What other questions do you have about implementing TRTW lessons?

Practice

1. Take turns sharing solutions for any additional questions that have surfaced.

2. Brainstorm other possibilities for "early finishers."

CHAPTER EIGHT
Sample Plans

The sample lessons in this section use various academic standards to demonstrate the TRTW framework.

They provide teachers with models of ways the TRTW approach can be used across content areas in K-12 classrooms.

LESSON INDEX

1. KINDERGARTEN SOCIAL STUDIES: WHY PEOPLE WORK

Talk #1
Why do your mom or dad work?

Read
Purpose: to find out why people work.
Shared reading of text with pictures; teacher reads first.
Students chorally read with the teacher second.

Talk #2
(Teacher models first and provides sentence stems.)

This is a _____. She/He helps _____.

Give partners pictures of other "workers" (ex: policewoman, principal of the school, waiter.)
Ask them to describe each worker using the stems for each picture.

Write
(Teacher models with example and then brainstorms a list of other examples
that students can use in their writing.)

Why do people work? Give one example.

People work because _____.
One example is _____.

ALIGNED TO THE
FOLLOWING STANDARDS:

Identify jobs in the home, school,
and community.

Explain why people have jobs.

Text

One reason people work is
to help the community.

Doctors help sick
people feel better.

 Mechanics
help fix cars.

Farmers help
grow food for
people to eat.

2. KINDERGARTEN MATH: 2-DIMENSIONAL SHAPES

Materials: Ziploc bag with 4 different 2-dimensional shapes (cut from different colored paper) – 1 per partnership; Anchor Chart

Talk #1

Ask partners to take turns pulling out a shape from the Ziploc bag and telling anything they know about that shape.

Read

Tell students our purpose for reading is to identify the attributes of 2-dimensional shapes. Chorally read each part of the anchor chart.

Talk #2

Model how to use the sentence stems. Ask partner A to pick a shape from the Ziploc and chorally repeat the stems for that shape to Partner B. Repeat the process with Partner B to Partner A.

Write

Ask each student to pick a shape and complete the sentence stems in their journal or on a dry erase board.

ALIGNED TO THE
FOLLOWING STANDARDS:

Identify 2-dimensional shapes.

Identify attributes of 2-dimensional shapes.

TALK #1

Tell what you know about each shape.

Text

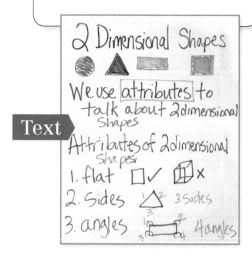

2 Dimensional Shapes

We use attributes to talk about 2 dimensional Shapes

Attributes of 2 dimensional Shapes:
1. flat ☐✓ ▱✗
2. Sides △ 3 sides
3. angles ▭ 4 angles

TALK #2

This shape is a _____.

One attribute is that it has ____ sides.

Another attribute is that it has ____ angles.

WRITE

_____ is a 2-dimensional shape.

I know because...

---

3. 1ST GRADE READING: RETELL BEGINNING, MIDDLE & END

Talk #1

Tell your partner what you did after school yesterday.

Read

Purpose: to identify BME in order to retell a story.

Read the anchor chart together. Teacher reads a part, then class rereads the same part all together.

Text ▶

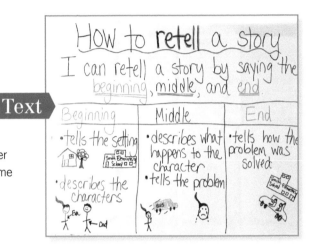

Talk #2

Partners use this graphic organizer to retell stories they have previously read as a class. They do not write anything, but use the sentence stems to guide their talking.

Beginning	Middle	End
In the beginning... The setting is... The main characters are...	The problem is... Some important events are...	In the end... The problem was solved...

Write

Teacher reads aloud a new story and asks students to listen carefully for the beginning, middle, and end. Students complete the graphic organizer for the story.

Beginning	Middle	End
In the beginning...	The problem is...	In the end...

ALIGNED TO THE FOLLOWING STANDARDS:

Retell the order of events in a text by referring to the words and/or illustrations.

Retell stories, including key details, and demonstrate understanding of their central message or lesson.

4. 1ST GRADE SCIENCE: LIVING/NON-LIVING THINGS

Talk #1
How are these two bears different?

Read
Purpose: to identify the characteristics of living and non-living things.

> The world is made up of living and non-living things. People, plants, and animals are living things. Living things eat and breathe. They also grow and move. Living things produce (make) new living things. For example, mothers produce babies. Non-living things do not need to eat and do not breathe. They do not grow or move. Examples of non-living things are teddy bears, rocks, and buildings.
>
> **Text**

Talk #2
1. How are living things and non-living things different?

2. Sort these pictures into living and non-living.
   (Teacher provides 4-6 pictures to each talking group.)

Living	Non-living

Write
Is a butterfly a living or non-living thing?
Give 2 reasons for how you know.

ALIGNED TO THE FOLLOWING STANDARD:

Sort and classify living and non-living things based upon whether or not they have basic needs and produce offspring.

5. 2ND GRADE ELAR: BIOGRAPHY

Talk #1

Name one famous person and tell what you know about that person.
Discuss with your partner: "_____ is a famous person. I know..."

Read

The text was created as a class during the previous lesson. Today's purpose for reading is to review the characteristics of a biography. Ask students to silently read the text for purpose.

Text ▶ *What is a biography?*

A genre of writing (like fiction or nonfiction)

A real story about a person's life

Usually about a notable person, describing their accomplishments and their life

Written by another person

Explains how the person affected others

Can be a book, TV show, documentary

Tells about their life in chronological order, like a timeline.

Talk #2

How can you determine if you are reading a biography?
Try to talk about at least 3 ways.

Stem:
One way I can determine if I am reading a biography is...
I know the text is a biography because...

Write

What are 3 characteristics of a biography?

Stem: *3 characteristics of a biography are...*

ALIGNED TO THE
FOLLOWING STANDARD:

Draw conclusions about genre in different contexts and provide evidence from the text to support sunderstanding.

6. 2ND GRADE READING: CHARACTER RESPONSE

Talk #1

How would you feel if you found out that you were moving away from where you live right now?

If I found out that I was moving, I would feel _____ because…

Read

Purpose: to describe how Kimberly responds to challenges.

Kimberly was walking to school and she dropped her library book. It fell in a puddle of water. "Oh no!" she said. She picked up her book right away. She tried to wipe all the water off of it but every page was wet. She began to worry. What if her teacher yelled at her? What if the librarian got mad at her? She worried all the way to school.

In class, Kimberly hid the book in her desk because she was afraid to tell her teacher. When it was time to go to the library, the teacher asked all of the students to put their library books in the basket. Kimberly did not get up. Her teacher asked her where her library book was. Kimberly said, "I left it at home."

Text

Talk #2

What was Kimberly's challenge (problem)?

What was her response to the problem? (What did she do? How did she feel?)

If you were Kimberly, how would you respond?

Write

Do you agree or disagree with the way Kimberly responded to her problem? Why?

Paragraph frame:

Kimberly's problem was

_____.

I _____ with the way Kimberly responded because…

I think Kimberly…

ALIGNED TO THE FOLLOWING STANDARD:

Describe main characters in works of fiction, including their traits, motivations, and feelings.

7. 3RD GRADE MATH: PERIMETER

TALK #1

If Mrs. Blanco had to build a new fence around Terrace Elementary, how would she know how much material to buy?

Purpose: to identify how to calculate perimeter.

READ

Perimeter is the distance around an object or shape. In order to find the perimeter of an object or shape, we need to add all of the sides together. Here is an example:

6 ft
4 ft   4 ft
6 ft

6 ft
6 ft
4 ft
+4 ft
----
20 ft

I added all of the sides of this rectangle together to find the perimeter.

TALK #2

Explain how to find the perimeter of this square

8 ft
8 ft   8 ft
8 ft

WRITE

What is perimeter and how can you find the perimeter of an object?

ALIGNED TO THE
FOLLOWING STANDARD:

Determine the perimeter of a polygon.

8. 3RD GRADE ELAR: SIMILES

Talk #1

Imagine that you called your friend to come over and play, and he said, "I'll be there as quick as lightning." What does your friend mean?

Read

Purpose: to define simile.

> A simile is a phrase that compares two things that are alike in some way.
>
> Some similes include the word "as." For example, Jaelyn was as cute as a kitten. Jaelyn and a kitten are alike because they are both cute. Other similes include the word "like." For example, when the football player broke his arm, he was screaming like a baby. The football player was screaming so loudly that he sounded like a screaming baby.
>
> Using similes in your writing helps to make your story more interesting and entertaining for the reader.
>
> **Text**

Talk #2

With your group, try to create 5 similes using the words "like" or "as." Remember you are comparing two things that are similar.

Write

Look back at your rough draft.
Add one simile to make your story more interesting.

ALIGNED TO THE FOLLOWING STANDARDS:

Demonstrate understanding of figurative language, word relationships, and nuances in word meanings.

Distinguish the literal and nonliteral meanings of words and phrases in context *(e.g., take steps).*

Talk #1

Brainstorm ideas for how to be safe in the lab with your partner. Try to generate 3 ideas.

Read

Purpose: to identify the rules for the lab. Highlight two key words for each rule.

Talk #2

Are there any other rules needed to keep us safe in the lab?

Why do you think rule _____ is necessary? (Start with Rule 7, 6, & 4)

Write

Which two rules do you think are the most important? Explain why.

Text

RULES FOR LAB SAFETY

1. I will not eat, drink, or taste anything in the lab unless approved by the teacher.

2. I will wear safety goggles when the teacher tells me it is necessary.

3. I will not run around or play during the time of an experiment.

4. I will not touch supplies and/or materials without permission and treat the lab equipment with care.

5. I will only conduct experiments approved by the teacher.

6. I will report any spills.

7. I will keep my hands away from my eyes and mouth during experiments.

8. I will listen carefully and follow directions.

ALIGNED TO THE FOLLOWING STANDARD:

Demonstrate safe practices during classroom and outdoor investigations.

10. 4TH GRADE READING: MAKING CONNECTIONS

Talk #1

If you could have any pet you wanted, what kind of pet would you have?
Tell your partner why.

Read

Purpose: to make connections to the text.

pp. 1-9 of *Tales of a Fourth Grade Nothing* by Judy Blume

Pay Attention To (PAT) List

Pat attention to the parts of the story where you make a connection.

• Do any parts remind you of yourself? (text to self)

• Do any parts remind you of any other books or stories you've read? (text to text)

• Do any parts remind you of something else? (text to world)

Talk #2: Check-in Conversation

With your group, take turns explaining the connections you made with the text.

1. Tell your group the page number and paragraph number of your connection.

2. Read the section out loud.

3. Tell your connection.

4. Discuss if that connection is a TS, TT, or TW.

5. Repeat with next group member.

Write

Tell about a connection you made to the story. Summarize the part of the story, then explain how you connected with it. Tell whether your connection was text to text, text to self, or text to world.

ALIGNED TO THE FOLLOWING STANDARDS:

Read grade-level text with fluency and comprehension.

Make connections and provide evidence from the text to support their understanding.

11. 5TH GRADE MATH: MULTIPLE STEP PROBLEM

TALK #1

Talk with your partner about what this is.
Does it have any special meaning?

READ and solve in your journal

Audrey spent all summer making friendship bracelets. She had 185 once school started. She gave 25 bracelets to her best friend and put the rest of the bracelets into containers. Each bag contained 40 friendship bracelets. Which equation can be used to find **c**, the number of containers of bracelets Audrey had?

A. c = (185+25)+40   C. c = (185+25)×40
B. c = (185-25)x40   D. c =(185-25)÷40

TALK #2

With your partner, discuss:

Do your answers match?
Explain how you know that your answer is correct.

WRITE

Explain how you solved the problem.

Use the following mathematical terms as needed:

Add, subtract, multiply, and divide

ALIGNED TO THE
FOLLOWING STANDARD:

Represent and solve multi-step problems involving the four operations with whole numbers using equations with a letter standing for the unknown quantity.

12. 5TH GRADE SOCIAL STUDIES: WESTWARD EXPANSION

TALK #1

Think then Discuss

What makes a country greater: having more land or having more people?

submitted by
Cathlin Shahriary, Lewisville ISD

Pre-READ

How can we be better Social Studies readers?

- What are some strategies we can use to help us read and understand Social Studies text?
- Preview the text & examine vocabulary

READ

Your purpose for reading is to discover the different ways Americans acquired the land that is now the United States.

Pay attention to:

- How we acquired the land (was it through an agreement, a battle/war, purchase, or some other way)
- Where the land was located
- Which acquisition you think was most important

Text

pp. 255-261 *Social Studies Alive! America's Past* by Teacher's Curriculum Institute.

Envelope, Please! Questions

1) Choose one land acquisition and discuss how America would be different without that acquisition today.

2) Could it have stopped us from expanding in other directions or to other places?

3) Which land acquisition do you think was most important? Why?

4) Why did Americans think it was important to acquire more land?

TALK #2

Envelope, Please!

Use the questions in the envelope to guide a discussion with your table group. When you finish, I will randomly select a person from each group to share his/her thoughts and ideas.

WRITE

Make a Claim with Evidence

Write a short paragraph explaining which land acquisition you think was most important to our country and why. Make sure to use evidence from the text to support your claim. Focus on what made it more important than the others.

ALIGNED TO THE FOLLOWING STANDARD:

Identify significant events and concepts associated with U.S. territorial expansion.

13. 6TH GRADE SOCIAL STUDIES: LIMITED/UNLIMITED GOVERNMENT

Talk #1
Unlimited means

Can you think of something you would like to have an unlimited amount of?

Can you think of something that would be bad if you had an unlimited amount of it?

Read
Purpose: compare the characteristics of limited and unlimited governments.

> **Text**
>
> In a limited government, there are laws that limit how much power the leader has. Limited government is set up so that the leaders cannot abuse or misuse their powers. This helps to protect the rights of individuals. The United States is an example of a limited government. It has a Constitution and Bill of Rights that tell the laws for the country. Both the leaders and the citizens must follow those laws. There are checks and balances built into limited government. This means the leader, the lawmakers, and the courts can never have all of the power. Citizens have many freedoms. For example, they can choose their own religions, own and sell property, and pick their own careers and hobbies.
>
> An unlimited government is very different. Leaders in an unlimited government usually have absolute power. This means one leader usually decides all of the rules. The people who live in a place with unlimited government have no way to change the rules or limit the power of the leader. The rulers are free to do whatever they want. The people cannot make their own choices. The leaders often rule all areas of each person's life. The people lose many or all of their freedoms.

Talk #2
Are there any disadvantages to having limited government? Explain your thinking.

Why should the power of a government be limited?

Is our school run with limited or unlimited power? Explain your thinking.

Write
Would you rather live in a country with limited government or unlimited government? Please give at least 3 specific reasons for your choice.

ALIGNED TO THE
FOLLOWING STANDARD:

Government. Compare the characteristics of limited and unlimited governments.

Talk, Read, Talk, Write **SAMPLE PLAN**

14. 6TH GRADE GRAMMAR: COMMA RULES

Talk #1

It's time to eat, Sara.

It's time to eat Sara.

Do these two sentence mean the same thing? Please explain.

Read

Purpose: identify 10 comma rules.

While you are reading, highlight the comma in each example (see text on next page).

Talk #2

With your partner pull out one strip at a time and discuss two things:

1. Is the sentence correct or incorrect? If incorrect, identify where the comma(s) belong.

2. Which comma rule is being illustrated in the sentence?

When you finish with one strip, pull out the next and repeat.

Write

Reread your last two drafts from your writing folder. Find at least 3 sentences that have commas used correctly, or where you need to edit for commas. Highlight the sentences, correct them if needed, and write a 1-sentence explanation of why you need a comma in the sentence. (Use the comma rules chart to help you explain.)

ALIGNED TO THE FOLLOWING STANDARD:

Edit drafts for grammar, mechanics, and spelling.

Strips (need to be copied, cut apart, and placed in an envelope)

My dream vacation is to visit Anchorage Alaska.
Wow I can't believe it!
Why don't you eat some more Kelly?
World War II ended on May 8, 1945.
I ran two miles and I did 40 push-ups.
Francisco hollered "Time is up!"
The only channels we get on our TV are NBC CBS ABC and Fox.
After looking at all the reports, I think we need to change our plan.
The highest scoring class Mrs. Chapman's class won the popcorn party.
Dear Dad, Please don't forget to leave the gate open. Love Griffin

6TH GRADE GRAMMAR: COMMA RULES

Text

We need commas in order to make sense of sentences. Commas let the reader better understand the meaning of your writing. Here are some of the most common rules for commas:

Number	Rule	Example
1	Series To separate words in a list or series	I like salad, steak, and broccoli.
2	Dates To separate the day and year	I was born on June 21, 2006.
3	Location To separate the city and state	I live in Los Angeles, California.
4	Quotation To introduce or separate a short quotation	Mom shouted, "Get downstairs right now!" "Let's line up," said Mrs. Street, "it is time for electives."
5	Conjunction Before a conjunction (ex: and, but)	My sister ate all of her ice cream, but she forgot to clean up her bowl and spoon.
6	Names Before or after a person's name	Johnny, come here. Why didn't you ask me, Trina?
7	Qualifications To give additional information about a noun	The best amusement park in the world, Disneyland, is going to open in 5 minutes.
9	Greetings and Closings	Dear Mom, Sincerely, Paula
10	Introductory elements To separate words or phrases at the beginning of a sentence	Once upon a time, a little girl was born. Yes, I'd like another hot dog.

These are not all of the comma rules, but they will help you to improve your writing. They will also help you read with better understanding.

15. 7TH **GRADE SCIENCE:** HOMEOSTASIS

submitted by Edleen Aguilera-Nwachucu, San Elizario ISD

HOMEOSTASIS

Warm-up: Quick Write

How does your body respond to a foreign virus or bacteria? Why do you think your own body responds that way?

"When a foreign virus or bacteria invades my body, my body responds by..."

TALK #1

- Share your response with your shoulder partner.

- Come up with one more example in which your body responds that perhaps both of you may have missed.

READ

- 1st: I will model how I want you to read your article.
- 2nd: We will read it out loud as a class.
- 3rd: You will read the article on your own using your strategies (headings, vocabulary, etc.).

7TH GRADE SCIENCE: HOMEOSTASIS

AFTER YOU READ

- Show your headings to your partner and determine which is the best and discuss why.

TALK #2

- Open your envelopes and discuss each question with your shoulder partner using the sentence stems.

- Pop question: How does your endocrine system help regulate homeostasis?

Envelope, Please! Questions

1) How would your body react to the external stimulus of a pop quiz from your teacher with 5 minutes to complete?

"If a teacher gave me a pop quiz with 5 minutes to complete, my body's reaction would be to..."

2) How does your nervous system help maintain homeostasis in your body?

"The nervous system helps maintain homeostasis by..."

3) How would your body respond if you were stuck in the desert with little to no water?

"If I were stuck in the desert with little to no water my body would..."

4) Why do a plant's roots grow towards a water source?

"A plant's roots grow towards a water source because it is a(n) _____ stimulus and..."

5) Why does your body vomit? How does this reaction help maintain homeostasis?

"A body vomits in response to..."

ALIGNED TO THE FOLLOWING STANDARDS:

Investigate how organisms respond to external stimuli found in the environment.

Describe and relate responses in organisms that may result from internal stimuli that allow them to maintain balance.

WRITE

- Provide an example not already covered of an internal stimulus and an external stimulus. How does your body respond to the stimuli? How does it connect to homeostasis?

"An example of an internal stimulus is...."
"Your body responds to it by...."

Talk, Read, Talk, Write **SAMPLE TEXT**

7TH GRADE SCIENCE: HOMEOSTASIS

Name _____ Date _____ PD _____

Response: _____
_____
_____
_____

External and Internal Stimuli

1. Suppose you and your family take a camping trip to Colorado. Your father is trying to build a fire, and he asks you to collect some sticks. While you are searching, you encounter a huge bear. What is your immediate reaction? Run! This is a result of an external stimulus. An external stimulus is a stimulus that comes from outside an organism and causes a reaction. When you see the bear, your brain immediately recognizes danger. It triggers fear and the fight-or-flight response. You know that you cannot fight the bear and win. Your brain triggers the flight mode option, so that you can flee danger immediately.

2. Another example of an external stimulus is temperature. When it is cold outside, your response is to get warm by putting on a jacket. There are internal stimuli as well as external. An internal stimulus is a stimulus that comes from inside an organism. You may have experienced an internal stimulus of hunger after a long day at school. This stimulus prompts you to eat some food in order to regain needed energy.

3. An animal's response to stimuli is due to either learned behaviors or instinct. Learned behavior is a response to a stimulus that an animal was taught. Being able to read and write are examples of learned behavior, because it is not something you are born able to do. On the other end of the spectrum, instinct is a natural reaction to a stimulus that is automatic instead of taught. This can be seen especially in wildlife. All animals are capable of searching for food and water because of instinct.

4. Instinct and learned behaviors are responses that enable the body to survive. Without external and internal stimuli, your body would not be able to maintain homeostasis. Homeostasis is a property of organisms that regulates their internal environment, for example temperature or nutrient levels. Homeostasis tends to maintain a stable, constant condition despite changing external conditions. Basically, it keeps the body in balance with the environment. A good example of homeostasis can be seen in your own household: your thermostat. In the winter, you probably set your thermostat to about 75 degrees Fahrenheit to stay warm inside. Whenever the house temperature falls below 75 degrees, the thermostat will turn on the furnace to heat the house until it reaches the target temperature. This is similar to how the body works.

5. Homeostasis is regulated by a variety of receptors that monitor and respond to changes in a system, like your body. While playing a game of basketball, you may become very hot and produce sweat. This is a response to receptors that monitor body temperature so that it does not become too hot or too cold. Without these receptors and the mechanisms of homeostasis, your body could overheat. Temperatures that are too hot can destroy cells in your body, which could lead to death.

Text

6. All organisms must be able to maintain homeostasis. They do not all have the same homeostatic mechanisms as humans do, however. Plants cannot run away from bears because they do not have the fight-or-flight response that humans and animals have. The main need that plants have is getting enough water and sunlight. This is equivalent to a human's need for water and food. A special homeostatic mechanism that plants have is tropism, which is a growth response between a plant and an external stimulus. What kind of stimulus could this be? Examples are weather, touch, time, gravity, or light. There are two basic responses: positive and negative. A positive response is indicated by a plant's growth toward the stimulus. A negative response is when it grows away from the stimulus.

7. Two examples of tropism are gravitropism and phototropism. Gravitropism is a plant's growth response to gravity. Ideally, roots grow down in the ground to absorb water for a plant, and its stems and leaves grow upward above the ground to absorb light. If a plant were to lose its upright position, it may not be able to gain required nourishment. When this occurs, a plant will begin to bend so that it is upright once again. How is this possible? Plants have a special hormone called auxin that plays an important part in gravitropism. If the plant fell over, there would be increased levels of auxin on the lower side of its stem. This would stimulate cell elongation on the stem, causing the stem to bend toward the sky. At the same time, auxin also prohibits cell elongation in roots, which results in the roots bending down toward the soil. This special homeostatic mechanism gives the plant access to water and light no matter what its position.

8. Phototropism is a plant's response to light stimulus. It is also regulated by the plant hormone auxin. When the sun shines down on a plant, auxin will move to the darker side of the plant. This causes the cells on the dark side of the plant to elongate toward the sun. The other side of the plant remains the same. When the plant bends, it allows a larger amount of light to hit the surface of the leaves. The leaves are then able to absorb this light to begin conducting photosynthesis for food.

9. The human body is built to survive. However, our environment is constantly changing. Without homeostasis, the body would not be able to affectively adjust. Without homeostasis, there would be no internal stimuli to prompt you to eat when your body is lacking energy. There would be no mechanisms to keep your body temperature constant. You may get too hot or too cold. Plants would not be able to produce their own food without phototropism or gravitropism. Instinct and learned behavior both contribute to our essential homeostatic functions.

Write: _____

_____

_____

_____

Text

16. 7TH GRADE MATHEMATICS: PROBABILITY

Content Objective: Students will determine if a game is fair by creating a model, calculating probability, and explaining reasoning.

Talk #1: Make a Choice

There are two drawings for a free trip to New York. Contestants are only allowed to enter one of the drawings (not both), and they can only enter one time.

Drawing #1 will have exactly 50 names in the bucket.

Drawing #2 will have exactly 100 names in the bucket.

Would you enter your name in Drawing #1 or Drawing #2? Why?

Read: PAT List

Read "What are the chances of that?" Purpose: determine how to calculate the probability. (See following page for text.)

Pay Attention To (PAT) List

Probability

Outcome

Sample space

Simple event

Complementary event

How to determine fairness

Talk #2: Envelope, Please!

The following question is a sample envelope question:

Based on your knowledge from the Read section, calculate the odds in this question. Eleven people are racing. What are the odds of being first, second, or third?

Write: Clear Explanation

Jack and Jill are playing a game. There are 6 tiles in a box: 3 red and 3 blue. A player picks 2 tiles without looking. Jill gets a point if the tiles do not match; Jack gets a point if they do match. Write an explanation telling your teacher whether this is either a fair or unfair game.

ALIGNED TO THE FOLLOWING STANDARD:

Develop a probability model and use it to find probabilities of events. Compare probabilities from a model to observed frequencies; if the agreement is not good, explain possible sources of the discrepancy.

7TH GRADE MATHEMATICS: PROBABILITY

What are the chances of that?

You do not have to be a mind reader to answer that question. Anyone can use mathematics to determine the chance that an event will happen. This is called probability. Let's look at a specific example to explain more about probability.

Mr. Ramirez has a cup on his desk with pencils for students to use. There are 21 pencils in the cup, and 18 of them are sharpened. Three of his pencils have a broken tip. What are the chances that a student will pick a pencil that is broken?

In this example, there are 21 pencils that could be selected. The pencils are called outcomes. If we list all the outcomes, or each type of pencil, this is called the sample space. The sample space for this problem could look like this:

We will assume that each outcome happens at random, which means that students pick out a pencil by chance. They will not know ahead of time what type of pencil (sharpened or broken) they are selecting. Basically, this problem is asking about a simple event, or a specific type of outcome. The simple event, in this case, is a student selecting a broken pencil out of the cup. Probability is the chance that this simple event will happen.

How do we determine the probability that the event will occur? We compare the number of favorable outcomes (picking the broken pencil) to the number of possible outcomes (picking either a broken or a sharpened pencil).

$$\text{Probability} = \frac{3 \text{ number of broken pencils (favorable outcomes)}}{21 \text{ number of all pencils (possible outcomes)}} = \frac{1}{7}$$

The probability that a student will select a broken pencil is 1/7.

A probability can be expressed as a fraction, a decimal, or a percent. The probability that a student will select a broken pencil can be described at 1/7, or 0.14, or 14%.

The probability that an event will happen is between 0 and 1 inclusive.

General Guidelines for Probability	
Impossible	0.0. or 0%
Not Very Likely	0.25 or 25%
Equally Likely	0.5 or 50%
Somewhat Likely	0.75 or 75%
Certain	1.0 or 100%

Text

7TH GRADE MATHEMATICS: PROBABILITY

What are the chances of that? continued

Let's look at another example:

John has 4 nickels and 2 pennies in his pocket. If he randomly selects 2 coins from his pocket, what is the probability that the coins will total exactly 6 cents?

The outcome in this problem is 2 coins. Take a minute and try to determine all of the possible outcomes, or the sample space. Once you have finished, compare your list to the one below.

4 Nickels = N1, N2, N3, N4
2 Pennies = P1, P2

$N1 + N2 = 10$				
$N1 + N3 = 10$	$N2 + N3 = 10$	$N3 + N4 = 10$		
$N1 + N4 = 10$	$N2 + N4 = 10$	$N3 + P1 = 6$	$N4 + P1 = 6$	
$N1 + P1 = 6$	$N2 + P1 = 6$	$N3 + P2 = 6$	$N4 + P2 = 6$	$P1 + P2 = 2$
$N1 + P2 = 6$	$N2 + P2 = 6$			

According to the sample space above, there are 8 combinations in the simple event of selecting 2 coins that total 6 cents. Another way to articulate this is: there are 8 favorable outcomes out of 15 possible outcomes.

The probability of selecting 2 coins that total 6 cents therefore is 8/15.

$$\text{Probability} = \frac{8 \text{ favorable outcomes}}{15 \text{ possible outcomes}}$$

The probability can also be expressed as a decimal (0.53) or a percent (53%).

Knowing the probability of a simple event allows observers to know the probability of the complementary event. The complementary event is the sum of outcomes that do not include the simple event. In the problem above, the complementary event includes all combinations of two coins that do NOT total 6 cents.

$$\text{Probability of the complementary event} = \frac{7 \text{ outcomes (2 coins that do NOT total 6 cents)}}{15 \text{ possible outcomes}}$$

The probability that 2 randomly selected coins will NOT total 6 cents = 7/15, or .47, or 47%.

The probability of a simple event and its complementary event will always add up to 1.

Determining the probability that an event will occur has many practical applications. For example, calculating the probability of various outcomes in games of chance like dominoes, cards, or dice will help you determine if the game is fair or not.

A game is fair when the favorable outcome and its opposite are equally likely to occur. In other words, a game is fair when the probability of both the simple event and its complementary event are exactly the same.

Text

17. 7TH GRADE WRITING: REAL-WORLD EXAMPLES

Content Objective: We will identify a real-world example of confidence by reading the "Kevin Hart" text.

Language Objective: We will write about a real-world example using:
"One person I feel is confident is …"
"_____ displays confidence because…"

Talk #1

https://www.youtube.com/
watch?v=AARlmX4Du7Q

Ask: What does it mean to be confident?

Stem: *Confidence means…*

Read

"How is Kevin Hart Confident?"

Pay Attention To (PAT) List

Find 3 words or phrases that show confidence

Determine the meaning of self-deprecation

Talk #2

1. Do you agree that you should call out your own flaws so a person can be taken seriously?

• *I agree because…*

• *I disagree because…*

2. Can you think of a real-world person who is confident? How can you tell?

• *One real-world person who is confident is _____ because…*

• *I can tell when someone has confidence because…*

Write

Select a person who you feel is confident. Explain why and give at least one specific example from the real world. (3-5 sentences)

• *One person I feel is confident is…*

• *_____ displays confidence because…*

Text

When we include real-world examples in our writing, it shows that we can connect a topic to something bigger than our own life. Using ideas and details from many different sources shows that we can organize and develop our thinking. The more connections you can make, the stronger your writing will be.

Today we are learning about the importance of confidence. You probably have many examples of times in your own life when you have been confident. Here is a real-world example of a person who shows confidence.

Funnyman Kevin Hart may be lacking in height, but he certainly isn't short on confidence. When the comedian and actor appeared on "Oprah Prime," he told Oprah he's "beyond confident" about his stature.

"I don't believe in doing things to manufacture my body to appeal to what I think people might like," Hart says in the above video. "This is it. This is what I was given. This is my playing cards. If we were playing poker, I've got to make this hand work. This is it for me. And this is what I'm going to ride out. So how do you not embrace it? You get one life. One. You get one life. I'm going to embrace mine."

Oprah asks if he was picked on for his height as a child, but Hart says he had a strategy. "I did it before they did," he says. "Self-deprecation."

It's a technique he still uses today. "Anything that the person thinks that they can say, I disarm you of it by saying it myself," Hart says.

His height has been the butt of jokes in movies like "Think Like a Man," "About Last Night," and "Ride Along," but Hart says he addresses it so the focus can turn to his acting.

"Take me seriously," Hart says. "Take me and my role seriously. Take my talent seriously."

"Oprah Prime" airs Sundays at 9 p.m. ET on OWN.

ALIGNED TO THE FOLLOWING STANDARD:
Write literary texts to express ideas and feelings about real or imagined people, events, and ideas.

Talk, Read, Talk, Write **SAMPLE PLAN**

18. 8TH GRADE READING: MOOD

Content Objective: We will analyze the mood of "The Monkey's Paw" by discussing words/phrases that generate emotion.

Language Objective: We will explain our thinking using:

I can infer that the mood is_____. The words "_____" make me think...

Talk #1

What is the mood?

I can infer the mood is _____ because...

Read

Read lines 200-229 on p. 384 of "The Monkey's Paw" in order to identify the mood of this section.

Source for the "The Monkey's Paw": *Holt McDougal Literature,* Grade 8, Texas Edition (2010).

Write down any words or phrases that help you generate emotion.

Talk #2

What is the mood? How do you know?

- *I can infer that the mood is _____ because...*
- *The words "_____" make me think...*
- *When I read "_____" I feel...*
- *Other words that help me infer that the mood is _____ are...*

Write

What is the mood? How do you know?

I can infer that the mood is _____. The words "_____" make me think...

ALIGNED TO THE FOLLOWING STANDARD:
Draw conclusions about elements of fiction and provide evidence from text to support understanding.

19. 8TH GRADE ELAR: INFER CHARACTER TRAITS

Content Objective: We will infer the protagonist's dominant trait by selecting words from the text and discussing the images those words create in our minds.

Language Objective: We will describe our inferences in writing using specific words from the text. "One phrase that helps me infer _____ is ..."

Talk #1

How would you describe this person?

What words make you think that?

> He was a friendly presence on billboards and in advertisements and on The New Girl. He regularly attended numerous charity and community outings. And his wholesome, boyish looks—somewhat at odds with his hulking frame—indicated it was all coming from a genuine place.

Excerpt from Valdez, Andrea. "The Watt Age." *Texas Monthly*, August 15, 2015.

Read

Read excerpt from *Dust Tracks on a Road* in order to answer:
• How would you describe the protagonist?
• What words make you think that?

Pay Attention To (PAT) List

1st and last paragraphs

Protagonist's thoughts

Protagonist's actions

Excerpt taken from *Holt McDougal Literature*, Grade 8, Texas Edition (2010).

Talk #2

What is the protagonist's dominant character trait?

How does the author's diction help you to infer this trait?

Write

On a piece of notebook paper:

1. Select a word or phrase from the excerpt of *Dust Tracks on a Road* and explain how it helps you to know that the protagonist is obstinate.

2. Select a different word or phrase to explain how it also shows that the protagonist is obstinate.
   "One phrase that helps me infer _____ is..."

4-6 sentences

ALIGNED TO THE FOLLOWING STANDARD: Make inferences about the elements of fiction and provide evidence from text to support understanding.

20. 8TH GRADE SCIENCE: LAW OF CONSERVATION OF MASS

Content Objective: I will relate the law of conservation of mass to balanced chemical equations by reading pp.125-126 and discussing them with my partner.

Language Objective: I will write my thinking using:
"Balanced chemical equations relate to the law of conservation of mass because..."

Talk #1

Which grade did a better job of fundraising?

7th Grade	8th grade
Ms. Anthony	Ms. Alexander
Mr. Willey	Mr. Jeffry
Ms. Rebeles	Ms. Frankum

I think _____ did a better job fundraising because...

Read

Complete guided notes

Purpose: to explain law of conservation of mass. Read p.125.

Purpose: to explain how to recognize if a chemical equation is balanced. Read p.126.

Talk #2

1. Is this equation balanced? Explain why or why not?

   $Mg + 2H2O = Mg(OH)2 + H2$

   This equation is _____ because...

2. *This equation relates to the law of conservation of mass because...*

Write

Balanced chemical equations relate to the law of conservation of mass because...

WORD BANK:	
Atoms	Reactants
Coefficient	Product
Mass	Equal

ALIGNED TO THE FOLLOWING STANDARD:

Recognize whether a chemical equation containing coefficients is balanced or not, and how that relates to the law of conservation of mass.

submitted by Allison Ventuo,
owner of Ducks in a
Row Personal Organizing

21. HIGH SCHOOL AVID: SYLLABUS

Talk #1

If you could bring only 3 school supplies with you on the first day of college, what would you bring and why?

Response stem: *On the first day of college, I would bring _____ because _____.*

Read

Read the sample syllabus in order to determine what information it provides.

Pay Attention To (PAT) List

As you read, please annotate:

1. How the information is organized

2. Any questions you have for the professor and/or TA

Talk #2

Divide the room into sections of the syllabus.

Think time: Which 2 sections of the syllabus are the most important? Please refer to the syllabus for your support.

Action time: Please stand in the section of the room you think is most important. Form a pair and discuss.

Response stem:
The ___ is one of the most important sections of the syllabus because ___.

(Repeat with the second most important section.)

Write

Explain what you will have to do to be successful in a college class. Where in the syllabus is helpful information located?

Smith College Course Syllabus – Fall 2015
Course Title: College 101

Course Description: Assist students with the transition to college through coursework on prioritization, campus involvement, study skills, etc.

Course Credit Hours: 3

Withdrawal Policy: Please refer to the current student handbook.

Administrative Withdrawal: Failure to fully participate in the class may result in an administrative withdrawal. Please refer to the current student handbook.

Repeat Policy: Failure to successfully complete the course may result in negative scholastic and financial consequences. You may only repeat this course one time. Please refer to the current student handbook for additional information.

Smith College Academic Integrity Policies: Failure to uphold the academic integrity policies may result in removal from the class and/or Smith College. Please refer to the current student handbook.

Americans with Disabilities Act: Smith College will adhere to all relevant laws. Please refer to the current student handbook.

Instructor's Name: Allison Venuto
Office Number: A123
Office Hours: M/W from 8am until 10am or available by appointment
Phone Number: (555) 555-1234
Email: avenuto@sc.edu (best way to reach me; however, please expect a 24 to 48 hour turnaround on responses)

Class Meeting Times: M/W 10am – 11:15am
Class Meeting Location: A124
Course Resources: College 101 (2nd edition) by Allison Venuto

Attendance Policy: Students are expected to attend each class and to arrive on time. Being late (more than 5 minutes) or leaving early is an absence and will result in the student's attendance grade being lowered.

The instructor will not make decisions about the nature of absences. You are present or absent.

Attendance for this course will be determined as follows:
0 absence = 100 attendance points   1 absence = 90 attendance points
2 absences = 80 attendance points   3 absences = 70 attendance points
4 or more absences = 0 attendance points

Text

HIGH SCHOOL AVID: SYLLABUS

The final grade for this course will be based on the following criteria:

Attendance - 10%

Participation - 15%

Homework - 30%

Event Presentation – 15%

Final Exam - 20%

Final Exam Calendar – 10%

Total: 100%

Important Class Information:

All assignments must be typed. Failure to use proper grammar will result in a reduction of points.

Readings: Students are expected to complete assigned readings prior to coming to class.

Participation: Students are expected to participate in class activities and discussions.

Homework: Students are expected to complete and submit homework assignments. Late work will not be accepted.

Individual Conference: A critical component of this class will be a one-on-one conference with your instructor held during a prearranged class time.

Smith College Event: During this semester you will be required to attend at least one Smith College event and/or volunteer for 2 hours at a local nonprofit. The events must be sponsored by Smith College or a Smith College student organization. Please obtain approval of the event prior to attending and document your attendance through pictures.

Final Exam: On the day of the exam, students are asked to complete a comprehensive final exam consisting of true/false, multiple choice, and short answer questions.

Technology in Class: All technology must be turned off and put away as soon as you enter the classroom. Texting and surfing the Internet during class are considered rude and unacceptable and may result in withdrawal. No videos, pictures, or sound recordings may be made in class without first receiving the instructor's permission.

Text

Talk, Read, Talk, Write **SAMPLE TEXT**

Course Calendar
Topics/Assignments are subject to change.
(All changes will be announced in class and posted on Blackboard.)

	Come to class with: Read chapter 1
August 24	**August 31**
Introduction	Self-assessment activity
Syllabus and expectations	Chapter 1 lecture and activities
Blackboard introduction	Discuss Philosophy of Education
Annotate finances article	Marshmallow video and article

Come to class with:	**Come to class with:**
Article	Read Chapter 3 (through p. 118)
Read Chapter 2 (through p. 68)	
September 14	**September 21**
Philosophy of Education	Chapter 3 lecture and activities
Chapter 2 lecture and activities	Mindset video
Have to vs. choose to	
Communication with profs	Brain dump
Article discussion	Time audit

Come to class with:	**Come to class with:**
Read pp. 69–90 and pp. 119–138, Article	Chapter 4 (through p. 169)
September 28	**October 5**
Lecture and activities	Chapter 4 lecture and activities
Graph, picture, chart, map "lecture"	Article discussion
Annotate article	
Guest speaker – Advising	Forward planning

Text

HIGH SCHOOL AVID: SYLLABUS

Come to class with: Chapter 5 (through p. 218)	Come to class with: Having completed one on-campus activity When not meeting with me, will work in groups on presentation
October 12	**October 19**
Scavenger hunt	Individual conference, others project
Chapter 5 Lecture and activities	Individual conference, others project
Relationship bank account Set up a study group	Individual conference, others project

Come to class with: Read pp. 169 – 192 Read pp. 219 – 234	Come to class with: Chapter 6 (through p. 258)
October 26	**November 2**
Presentations on Smith College event	Chapter 6 Lecture and activities
Study Skills lecture	Discussion on pp. 236 and 244 – 5
Textbook marking	Self-defeating patterns

Come to class with: Read Chapter 7 (through p. 309) Annotated article	Come to class with:
November 16	**November 23**
Chapter 7 lecture and activities	No class due to Thanksgiving break
Article discussion	
Career Center Speaker	

Come to class with: Read pp. 268 – 280 Read pp. 310 – 330	Come to class with:
November 30	**December 7**
Lecture and activities	Final Exam
Multiple Choices	Final Exam
Library tour	

Text

Talk, Read, Talk, Write **SAMPLE PLAN**

22. HIGH SCHOOL GEOMETRY: EXTERIOR/INTERIOR ANGLES

Talk #1
How are angles used in real life?

Read
Purpose: determine how to calculate the measure of an exterior angle.

Talk #2: Partner Talk
What is the measure of the angle *n* on this triangle? Explain how you solved it.

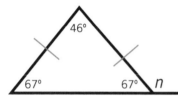

Write
Explain the relationship between interior and exterior angles.

ALIGNED TO THE
FOLLOWING STANDARDS:

Know precise definitions of angle, circle, perpendicular line, parallel line, and line segment, based on the undefined notions of point, line, distance along a line, and distance around a circular arc.

Use informal arguments to establish facts about the angle sum and exterior angle of triangles.

An interior angle is any angle on the inside of a polygon. An exterior angle is formed by extending one side of a polygon. It is the supplement of an interior angle of the polygon.

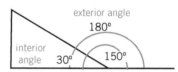

The sum of the interior angle and its corresponding exterior angle is 180 degrees.

The sum of the two opposite interior angles is equal to the exterior angle of the third angle. For example:

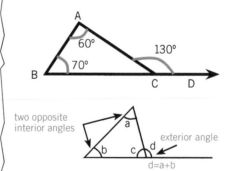

148 TALK, READ, TALK, WRITE

23. HIGH SCHOOL WORLD GEOGRAPHY: MIGRATION, PUSH/PULL FACTORS

Content Objective: Students will apply knowledge of social, political, economic, and environmental push/pull factors to explain the current immigration patterns of a nation.

Talk #1: Ask a Provocative Question

If you and your family could live somewhere else, where would you move? Think of at least three reasons why you would move to that location.

Read: Annotation

Read and annotate "Migration, Push/Pull Factors." (See p. 46 from the Read section for annotation instruction.)
Purpose: identify the factors that influence where and why people migrate.

Talk #2: Envelope, Please!

The following questions are sample envelope questions:

1) Which push factor is the most significant cause for migrating from a country?

2) Which pull factor is the most convincing reason to immigrate to a new country? Support your thinking with specific examples.

Write: Make a Claim with Evidence

According to the 2009 census, there are approximately 38.5 million immigrants in the United States. The top four source countries are: Mexico (30%), the Philippines (4.5%), India (4.3%), and China (3.7%). Pick one of the four source countries. Which one of the following categories do you think is the most significant consideration for people who immigrate to the United States from that country: political factors, economic factors, social factors, or environmental factors?
Your task is to write a compelling argument to convince your history teacher to believe your opinion is the correct way of thinking. The effective use of textual evidence and thoughtful reasoning is required.

ALIGNED TO THE FOLLOWING STANDARDS:

Explain the economic, political, and social factors that contribute to human migration.

Explain how international migrations are shaped by push/pull factors (e.g., political conditions, economic incentives, religious values, family ties).

Migration, Push/Pull Factors

People move from one place to another for many different reasons. This movement is called human migration. Sometimes it is over long distances, and it can involve large groups of people. Migration occurs because people either want to leave the conditions in which they currently live (push factors), or they desire to live somewhere that offers better conditions (pull factors). People often migrate for a combination of both push and pull factors. For example, a person might move from New York to Houston in order to get away from the cold winters (push factor) or because the cost of living is lower in Houston (pull factor). There are innumerable reasons for human migration. They can be political, economic, social, and environmental factors.

Political factors that influence migration include war, instability, and injustice. Migration is high in war-torn countries because people try to escape the fighting, violence, and loss of life that characterizes war. While some countries are at war with other nations, many modern countries are at war within their own nations, much like Afghanistan and Egypt. In these countries, different ethnic, social, or cultural factions rise up against one another. Their purpose is to gain control of the government or to overthrow the government, as was the case in Egypt in 2011. These internal battles often lead to unstable political situations, and there is no consistent leadership to maintain control of the country. Residents of such nations often leave because control of power is constantly changing. Another significant political factor that affects migration patterns is the way the government rules. When rulers of a nation oppress its people by denying their individual rights or eliminating

their personal freedoms, citizens migrate in search of more just and fair places to live. Groups of people who emigrate from countries for the abovementioned political push factors immigrate to countries that offer an improved political climate. Political factors that pull people toward a new location include peace and stability, a fair court system, and a government that guarantees individual rights and freedoms.

Economic factors also play a significant role in a person's decision to live in a different place. Many people move because of money. Either they cannot make enough in their current location, or they think they can make more in a different location, or both. Poverty and limited job opportunities are common economic push factors. One historical example of migration was the Great Migration of African Americans from the south to the north between 1910-1920; this was due, in part, by economic factors. There were limited jobs for African Americans in the South, and they were low paying. Many migrated north to work in the factories and industrial plants for much higher wages. More job opportunities, higher salaries, and a lower cost of living are significant economic factors that pull people toward a new location.

The way the people interact with one another within a country or region can also be a reason for migration. Social factors such as oppression based upon race, ethnicity, sex, or lifestyle can create a dire situation. Many women in countries such as Afghanistan are unhappy with the limited opportunities available to females and want more control over their lives. Some countries have a state religion, and those who do not believe in the established religion migrate for free-

Text

Migration, Push/Pull Factors continued

dom of religion. People who migrate for social factors move to locations that offer personal freedom and social equality. They want to live in a country where they are afforded the same rights and privileges as those around them, regardless of race, ethnicity, gender, or lifestyle.

Environmental factors, such as natural disasters, pollution, radiation, drought, and undesirable climates, are other reasons for people to move from one place to another. Many Japanese have emigrated because of hazards related to radiation exposure. Some island residents, such as Haiti, move because of risks related to hurricanes and floods. Countries plagued with long-term drought, such as Ethiopia and Somalia, see increasing numbers of people emigrating due to food shortages. Undesirable weather can also influence migration. We see this phenomenon in the United States when many residents in

northern states move to southern states during the winter months to avoid the harsh conditions and bitter cold.

Humans migrate for a wide variety of political, economic, social, and environmental reasons. These push and pull factors prompt travel from one location to another. Physical geography affects the route and flow of human migration. Throughout history, human migration has followed the path of least resistance, and the route with the least number of barriers has the greatest pull factor. People usually migrate through valleys and along bodies of water rather than through mountain ranges, forests, or deserts. Migration to neighboring areas is much easier than moving across the world, and traveling to urban areas is more convenient than traveling to isolated areas. No matter the distance, migration has always been part of the human condition.

Text

24. 10TH GRADE ENGLISH: PERSUASION/ARGUMENT

Content Objective: Students will identify and emulate the techniques an author uses to convince the reader to accept a certain point of view.

Talk #1: Respond to a Visual

Look at these two photos. Which is more effective? Why?

1 in 3 children born in 2000 will develop Type II diabetes, which leads to increased risk of heart disease, and decreases life expectancy by up to 22 years. That one child could be you.

Mary has Type II diabetes. She has chronic foot numbness, suffers from depression, battles skin infections and her blood pressure is so high that she worries about dying from a heart attack.

Read: Highlighting PLUS

Read "How do authors convince their readers?" Your purpose for reading is to identify how authors make an appeal to their readers. Based on the reading, determine which type of appeal is most effective when writing to persuade.

As you read, highlight words, phrases, or sentences that support your purpose for reading. Highlight at least 3 items. Be prepared to discuss the highlighted items in triad groups after reading.

Talk #2: Check-in Conversation

In triads, take turns discussing the high-lighted sections. After group members have explained their reasons for highlighting, discuss/create other examples of the 3 types of appeals mentioned in the text.

Write: Clear Explanation

Explain the difference between persuasion and argument. Illustrate the difference by writing a statement from each genre to support this claim:

All high school graduates should go to college.

ALIGNED TO THE FOLLOWING STANDARD:

Write arguments to support claims in an analysis of substantive topics or texts using valid reasoning and relevant and sufficient evidence.

How do authors convince their readers?

Authors use a wide variety of techniques to convince readers to think the same way they do. Generally these appeals can be classified into three categories: ethos, pathos, and logos.

Ethos is an appeal to ethics. An author who uses ethos to persuade his readers does so by building his own good character and credibility. He wants the reader to view him as trustworthy. Look at this example:

- *During all of my 32 years of marriage, one thing I know for sure is that communication is key.*

The author states the number of years he has been married as a way to convince the reader that he has the authority, or expert knowledge, to be viewed as a credible source on marriage.

Pathos is an appeal to emotion. Authors try to draw an emotional response from the reader as a way to persuade them. Sometimes the author appeals to positive emotions, as in,

- *We are all in this together because we care about our children. When we reach our fundraising goal, just imagine how our students will smile when they see the new playground.*

The author uses the positive images of students happily playing to make the reader feel joyful about donating money for a new playground. Authors also appeal to negative emotions as a way to get readers to take action, as in,

- *If we do not vote against Proposition 15, not only is the school budget at risk, but our teachers' jobs, and most importantly, our students' education is in jeopardy.*

The author hopes readers will feel so distressed and even fearful enough about their children's education that they will be eager to vote.

Logos is an appeal to reason and logic. Unlike ethos and pathos, this appeal is based on facts and statistics, rather than opinions and emotions. When using this approach, authors support their opinions by using evidence and reasoning. Some examples of logos include:

- *We should consider investing in this product because it has experienced over 8% increase in sales every quarter since it came on the market.*

- *By saving my babysitting money, I have twice as much money as I need to buy my new phone.*

- *Our campus does not want to change the schedule. In fact, 592 of 612 students interviewed stated they preferred the original schedule with a later start time.*

In each of the above examples, the authors provide support for their positions by offering numbers that are logical and irrefutable.

Text

10TH GRADE ENGLISH: PERSUASION/ARGUMENT

SELECTING AN APPROPRIATE APPEAL: PERSUASION VS. ARGUMENT

There are two types of writing that give the author a chance to persuade the reader: persuasion and argument. Persuasion appeals to the emotions of the reader. Argument appeals to logic and reason. Persuasive arguments are tailored for a specific audience, and primarily rely on ethos. It is critical for persuasive writers to consider the reader in order to make a connection and to establish credibility. Conversely, when writing an argument, it is critical for the author to present his claim and support it with reasoning logical enough to convince any audience. Effective arguments rely on logos to establish a universal common ground, and those kinds of arguments are supported with research and statistics.

HOW TO BUILD AN EFFECTIVE ARGUMENT?

While both methods of persuasive writing are useful in various contexts, in an academic setting, argument is the most commonly used approach to support a claim. Learning how to write an effective argument in high school will better prepare students for the type of writing they will be responsible for in college and throughout their careers. The key features of an effective argument include a clearly stated claim (thesis), evidence and reasoning, concessions and refutations, and a formal tone.

FEATURES OF AN EFFECTIVE ARGUMENT	
Claim/Thesis	A claim or thesis is a clear statement of the author's position on a debatable topic.
	What point of view is the author trying to get the reader to accept?
Evidence/Reasoning	Evidence and reasoning are facts, research, statistics, and universal common ground that support the claim.
	What are the logical reasons for the reader to accept the claim?
Concessions/Refutations	Concessions are acknowledgement of opposing claims. Refutations are an explanation of why those claims are invalid.
	What counterarguments can be made about the author's claim?
	Why are the counterarguments faulty/wrong/false, etc.?
Formal Tone	In writing, a formal tone is academic in nature, and it includes the use of precise language. A conversational tone and slang are absent from the text.
	Does the author communicate in a clear and academic way?

Text

25. HIGH SCHOOL BIOLOGY: BIOMOLECULES

Content Objective: Students will explain how the structure and function of biomolecules affect human life.

Talk #1: Make a Choice

If you were an elite athlete, would you rather eat a high protein/low carbohydrate diet, or would you rather eat a diet with equal amounts of carbohydrates and proteins? After you have made your decision, give two reasons to support your choice.

Read: PAT List

Read the text using the PAT List below. Purpose: analyze the structures and functions of the four types of biomolecules.

Pay Attention To (PAT) List

- 2 reasons why carbon is important
- For protein, carbohydrates, lipids and nucleic acid:
  - Name of subunits
  - At least 2 functions

Talk #2: Envelope, Please!

The following questions are sample envelope questions:

1) How is the structure and function of the four types of biomolecules the same?

2) What are the differences among the four types of biomolecules?

Write: Clear Explanation

Select two biomolecules and explain how the structure and function of each type of biomolecule helps support and sustain life. Write your explanation for a fellow biology student. Be sure to explain the two biomolecules carefully.

ALIGNED TO THE FOLLOWING STANDARD:

Compare the structure and functions of different types of biomolecules, including carbohydrates, lipids, proteins, and nucleic acids.

Biomolecules

Biomolecules are the building blocks of life; they make up every living thing. Breaking down the word biomolecule can help determine its meaning: bio means life, and a molecule is a group of atoms held together by bonds. Biomolecules, therefore, are groups of atoms that support and sustain life. Biomolecules are also referred to as organic molecules, organic compounds, and macromolecules. These terms can be used interchangeably to refer to the basic building blocks of life. Biomolecules are also called carbon compounds because each one is surrounded by a carbon skeleton, or backbone. Carbon is considered the most important element for all living things, from single celled organisms to multicellular plants and animals. There are two reasons. Carbon forms long lasting bonds that stabilize molecules; this means they are very strong. Additionally, carbon has many different bonding patterns, allowing for great variety within the molecules of life.

There are four basic biomolecules: proteins, carbohydrates, lipids, and nucleic acids. All four biomolecules are polymers that are composed of smaller building blocks, and each has specific functions that help sustain and support life.

Proteins are found in many food sources, and they serve several purposes. They are composed of amino acids that are linked together by a peptide bond. The shape of the protein molecule determines its function. It can include providing structure, transporting substances, and supporting chemical reactions. Proteins help give the shape and structure of cells within the body. For example, when the fibers within muscles begin to break down during exercise, they need proteins to repair the structural damage and to strengthen the form of each cell. Athletes and body builders usually include significant amounts of protein in their diet to ensure that their muscles have a well-defined structure. Proteins also transport substances in and out of the cell as needed, much like hemoglobin carries oxygen in our blood. Another function of proteins is to speed up chemical reactions. For example, some protein enzymes speed up the body's ability to break down starches in foods so the body can use them more efficiently.

A second type of biomolecule is a carbohydrate. Like proteins, they are composed of smaller building blocks. The subunits of carbohydrates are simple sugars, or saccharides. The functions of carbohydrates include: short-term energy supply, structure and support to cells, and cell recognition. Primarily carbohydrates provide cells with quick energy that can be used immediately. For example, when we eat foods with carbohydrates or something sugary like candy, we usually become energetic for a short period of time afterward. Carbohydrates also provide structure in the cell walls of plants, enabling plants to grow straight and tall. They also add structure in the hard exoskeleton of some crustaceans, like lobsters. The last function of carbohydrates is cell

Text

Biomolecules continued

recognition. Just like we recognize our friends by looking at their faces, cells can recognize each other by looking at the shapes and types of carbohydrates on the outside of the cell.

Lipids are another type of biomolecule that supports living things. Lipids are fats, oils, and waxes found within cells. The building blocks of lipids are simple carbon and hydrogen atoms. Lipids are used for long-term energy storage, insulation of our organs, and they also serve as a water barrier for cells. The energy from carbohydrates that is not used changes into lipids for storage. Because lipids (oils and fats) are insoluble in water, they are stored in the cell walls; they prevent water from entering or exiting the cell when it is unwanted.

Nucleic acid is the final biomolecule. It is the molecule that makes each living thing unique. Just like all other biomolecules, nucleic acids are made up of smaller units. In this case, they are called nucleotides. The function of some nucleic acids, like DNA and RNA, is to store genetic information. Another type of nucleic acid, ATP, is responsible for storing and releasing energy at the cellular level.

All four types of biomolecules are necessary for living organisms. Proteins, carbohydrates, lipids, and nucleic acid are all molecules that are composed of smaller building blocks. Each of these biomolecules serves a specific function to help sustain life for plants and animals.

Text

26. HIGH SCHOOL SPANISH 2/2H

submitted by
Amy Leonard, Plano ISD

Spanish 2/2H

Crimen y consecuencias
¿Cuál historia es mas justa?

LEARNING TARGETS:

I can make connections between behavior choices and their consequences.

I can give opinions and preferences and ask about those of others.

I can talk about a past event based on a prompt.

Conversación 1

Thinking Time (30 Seconds)

- No talking. Think and decide on your answer.
- Touch your nose when you have your answer.

Conversation 1 in ENGLISH (4 minutes)

- 1 minute per person
- Teacher times the intervals
- Partner 1 shares first, then 2, etc.

TOPIC: How have you been treated unfairly in the past? Describe the situation.

Antes de leer

See Scavenger Hunt on page 162.

Pre-reading Scavenger Hunt (3 minutes)

- Work collaboratively in your groups to match the Spanish word cards to the English word cards.
- Ask your teacher to check your work.

When you finish…

- Snap a pic with your phone to create your own cheat sheet to use during your reading.

HIGH SCHOOL SPANISH 2/2H

Leer

Text: Joven con "affluenza" quedó libre;
un inmigrante pobre no" — El Comercio, Lima

Purpose: Read this news article to...

A. Identify what crime the two young men committed and the consequences of their actions.

B. Make an inference as to why the young men faced different consequences.

C. Use your PAT List to indetify key words.

See PAT List
on page 163.

Después de leer

Group Processing - Check-in Conversation (4 minutes)

1. Use English here.

2. Check in with your table mates and compare results gathered during your reading on your PAT List.

3. Adjust your answers or help each other as needed.

Después de leer

Group Processing –
Graphic Organizer: (6 minutes)
Collaborate with your group to complete the graphic organizer.

List as many of the consequences each of the boys faced that you can.
Recommendation: List them in Spanish.

HIGH SCHOOL SPANISH 2/2H

Conversación 2 – Parte B

Parte B – Envelope, Please! (6 minutes) USE SPANISH NOW

1. Person 4 at each table, grab the envelope.

2. Person 4 pulls out one question at a time and read the question to your group.

3. Whole group then discusses the question until you feel you have exhausted all thoughts or points of view.

4. Person 4 pulls out another question, and the group continues the conversation.

NOTE: Don't worry about finishing all the questions.

Envelope, Please! Questions

1) ¿Piensas que "affluenza" es real? ¿Por qué o por qué no?

2) En tu opinión, ¿Por qué recibieron los dos jóvenes consecuencias diferentes?

3) ¿Cómo afecta una persona la falta o absencia de consecuencias?

4) En tu opinión, ¿Cuáles consecuencias son apropiadas para cada joven?

5) ¿Cuáles son las consecuencias indirectas para cada chico que no están mencionadas para cada chico?

Escribir / Exit Ticket

Task: Write an email to the newspaper editor in which you give your honest opinion about what true justice should look like for both young men. Support your position with specific details and points from your reading.

Audience: The editor of the newspaper, *El Comercio, Lima*

Self Assessment Tools (12 minutes*)

VOCABULARY	**Breadth of Vocabulary**	No evidence of Oops	Uses non-relevant vocabulary without significant use of the current group.	Uses little or repetitive vocabulary from current group.	Uses a variety of vocabulary from the current group.
	Text Type	No evidence of Oops	Uses lists of words or formulaic phrases only; 0-1 flavoring, sequencing &/or transition words appropriate to task.	Uses formulaic phrases & some simple sentences with little flavoring, sequencing &/or transition words appropriate to task.	Uses formulaic phrases & simple sentences with some personalization; a few flavoring, sequencing &/or transition words appropriate to task.

Resources

Associated Press. (2016, February 15). Joven con "affluenza" quedó libre; un inmigrante pobre no. Retrieved March 15, 2016, from http://elcomercio.pe/mundo/eeuu/joven-affluenza-quedo-libre-inmigrante-pobre-no-noticia-1879182

Adapted by Amy Leonard

HIGH SCHOOL SPANISH 2/2H

Pre-Reading Scavenger Hunt Manipulative | Teacher Instructions:

1. Print out one set of these.
2. Copy the target language cards on one color of cardstock, one set per student group.
3. Copy the English language cards on a different color cardstock, one set per student group.
4. Cut the words apart. Scramble them and place them in an envelope or Ziplock baggie.

EBRIO / EBRIED	FETO
ADINERADOS	DESVIAR
CONDUCTOR	RECHAZAR
TRIBUNAL JUVENIL	ACUERDO DE CULPABILIDAD
PERMANECER	LIBERTAD BAJO PALABRA

Pre-Reading Scavenger Hunt Manipulative | Teacher Instructions:

1. Print out one set of these.
2. Copy the target language cards on one color of cardstock, one set per student group.
3. Copy the English language cards on a different color cardstock, one set per student group.
4. Cut the words apart. Scramble them and place them in an envelope or Ziplock baggie.

INEBRIATED	FETUS
MONIED / WELL OFF	TO DEVIATE
DRIVER	TO REJECT
JUVENILE COURT	PLEA BARGAIN
TO REMAIN	PAROLE

HIGH SCHOOL SPANISH 2/2H

Nombre _____ Clase _____

Crimen y consecuencias: Dos historias

DURING READING TASK

The Pay Attention To List or PAT List

While You Read…
Pay attention to the terms you see below. What do you think they mean? Make your guesses here.

Paragraphs 1-2 Mataron / mató _____ Chocó contra _____ Embarazada _____	**Paragraph 8** Cargos _____ Permanence _____
Paragraph 3 Quedó libre _____	**Paragraph 11** Impedirle de manejar _____
Paragraph 4 Los fiscales _____	**Paragraph 14** Los testigos
Paragraph 6 Hirió de muerte _____ La conductora _____	**Paragraph 15** Salió volando _____ Sobrevivió _____
Paragraph 7 El juez _____ Rechazaría _____ Permaneció _____	**Paragraph 17** Será elegible _____

Nombre _____ Clase _____

Crimen y consecuencias: Dos historias
AFTER READING/GROUP PROCESSING TASK

Las consecuencias de crimen

1. Look over the *El Comercio* article called *"Joven con 'affluenza' quedó libre; un inmigrante pobre no"* again.

2. Look for and list all of the consequences you can find that each of the young men faced due to their crimes.

3. Recommendation: **List the consequences in Spanish.**

Jaime Arellano	Ethan Couch

27. HIGH SCHOOL ENGLISH: PROVIDE EVIDENCE

submitted by Katie Monaghan,
Dickinson ISD

Talk #1

Who motivates you?

"The individual that inspires me the most in life
is_____ because_____."

1. Write your answer on a note card.

2. Find your assigned partner. The tallest partner will read his/
   her sentence stem first. Shortest partner will read second.
   Decide which stem will be read to class.

Student Samples from Talk #1

> The individual that inspires and
> motivates me the most is my mommy
> because She dropped out of school
> when she was pregnant but went
> back an got her GED a few years
> later

> The individual that inspires and
> motivates me the most is my Dad
> because he always tried to get me
> to do the right things and helped
> me when i needed him to. All he
> wants is the best for me and he
> shows it.

Read

Purpose: to provide evidence from the text
to support your thinking.

Pay attention to:

1. How does Bilodeau regard his fellow Canadian competitors?

2. What does Alex want to do for his brother Frederic?

3. What does Alex say about his brother? Find at least 2 quotes.

Text: O'Conner, P. (2014, February 14). Canadian moguls skier
Alex Bilodeau dedicates gold to brother. *Student Daily News*.
Retrieved February 19, 2014, from www.studentdailynews.com

HIGH SCHOOL ENGLISH: PROVIDE EVIDENCE

Talk #2

1. Check in with your partner about the 3 questions.

2. Add additional information if your partner gives different text evidence.

Write

1. Let's discuss the reading and the characteristics of an inspirational person. (Whole class)

2. Write a personal narrative about an individual who motivates you. The sentence stem could be used as part of the introduction.

Sample of one student's narrative

(Narrative) My Inspiration

1. Since the yougest I could remeber
2. my family and I would always move
3. In and out of shelters to a motel
4. for the night. Since I was older
5. I understood things more then my
6. little brother. He grow up the way
7. I did not knowing what a real
8. life is like. Nobody in my family
9. has ever graduated. for the
10. longest time I was following my
11. my sisters food steps who had
12. just droped out of highschool and
13. got pregnet. when I tearnid fifth
14. teen I relized I wanted to
15. make a difference in my family

APPENDIX

TRTW Lesson Template

Standard:_____

Talk #1	Read
	Name of text: Purpose:
Possible Stems:	

Talk #2	Write
Possible Stems:	Possible Stems:

TRTW at a Glance

Overview of TALK #1	Strategies
Ask a Provocative Question	• Post a thought-provoking question related to the content concept. • Give students an opportunity to discuss answers with each other.
Make a Choice	• Post a situation or question that requires students to make a choice. • Ask students to explain and defend choices with each other.
Respond to a Visual	• Post an interesting or dramatic visual related to the content concept. • Ask students to share their thoughts about the visual with each other.
React to a Quotation	• Post a quotation that is connected to the content concept. • Ask students to describe their (or their partner's) reaction/response to the quotation.

Overview of READ	Strategies
PAT List	• Create a list of significant words, phrases, or ideas from the text. • Ask students to use that list while reading to ensure they understand important concepts.
Annotation	• Directly teach students ways to annotate. • Ask students to annotate while reading so they have a record of their thinking.
Highlighting PLUS	• Ask students to highlight important ideas from the text. • Give students the opportunity to refer to their highlighted text after reading, and have them explain why they highlighted it.

Overview of TALK #2	Strategies
Envelope, Please!	• Create 1-3 open-ended questions related to the text. • Give student groups open-ended questions in an envelope. • Ask groups to discuss answers to questions.
Check-in Conversation	• Give student groups an opportunity to discuss their annotations from the text. • Give student groups an opportunity to brainstorm ideas for writing.

Overview of WRITE	Strategies
Clear Explanation	• Give students a clear purpose and audience for their written explanation. • Provide students with Ways to Expand and Explain Thinking chart. • Analyze examples and non-examples of written explanations.
Make a Claim with Evidence	• Give students a clear purpose and audience for their claims. • Provide students with Ways to Expand and Explain Thinking chart. • Analyze examples and non-examples of claims with evidence.

QUESTION INDEX

BIBLIOGRAPHY

Achieve, Inc. (2005). *Rising to the challenge: Are high school graduates prepared for college and work?* Washington, DC: Author.

ACT. (2005). *Crisis at the core: Preparing all students for college and work.* Iowa City, IA: Author. Retrieved from files.eric.ed.gov/fulltext/ED493181.pdf

Adler, M. (1940). *How to read a book: The classic guide to intelligent reading.* New York, NY: Simon & Schuster.

Allen, J. (2000). *Yellow brick roads: Shared and guided paths to independent reading, 4-12.* Portland, ME: Stenhouse.

Appleby, J., et al. (2003). *The American vision.* New York, NY: Glencoe McGraw-Hill.

Beers, K., Probst, R.E., & Rief, L. (Eds.). (2007). *Adolescent literacy: Turning promise into practice.* Portsmouth, NH: Heinemann.

Biancarosa, C., & Snow, C.E. (2006). *Reading next –A vision for action and research in middle and high school literacy - A report to the Carnegie Corporation of New York* (2nd ed.).Washington, DC: Alliance for Excellent Education.

Daniels, H., & Zemelman, S. (2004). *Subjects matter.* Portsmouth, NH: Heinemann.

Echevarria, J., Vogt, M., & Short, D. (2008). *Making content comprehensible for English learners: The SIOP model.* Boston, MA: Pearson.

Ezzedeen, S. (2008). Facilitating class discussions around current and controversial issues: Ten recommendations for teachers. *College Teaching, 56*(4), 230-236.

Frey, N., & Fisher, D. (2011). Structuring the talk: Ensuring academic conversations matter. *The Clearing House, 84*, 15-20.

Gallagher, K. (2004). *Deeper reading: Comprehending challenging texts, 4-12.* Portland, ME: Stenhouse.

Goldenberg, C. (1992-1993). Instructional conversations: Promoting comprehension through discussion. *The Reading Teacher, 46*(4), 316-326.

Goldman, S. (2012). Adolescent literacy: Learning and understanding content. *Future Child, 22*(2), 89-115.

Graham, S., & Perin, D. (2007). *Writing next: Effective strategies to improve writing of adolescents in middle and high schools – A repost to the Carnegie Corporation of New York.* Washington, DC: Alliance for Excellent Education.

Harvey, S., & Goudvis, A. (2000). *Strategies that work: Teaching comprehension to enhance understanding.* York, ME: Stenhouse.

Henning, J. (2005). Leading discussions: Opening up the conversation. *College Teaching,* 53(3), 90-94.

Hoyt, L. (1999). *Revisit, reflect, retell: Strategies for improving reading comprehension.* Portsmouth, ME: Heinemann.

Kagan, S. (1994). *Cooperative learning.* University of Virgina: Kagan Cooperative Learning.

Keene, E. (2012). *Talk about understanding: Rethinking classroom talk to enhance comprehension.* Portsmouth, NH: Heinemann.

Marzano, R., Pickering, D., & Pollock, J. (2001). *Classroom instruction that works: Research-based strategies for increasing student achievement.* Upper Saddle River, NJ: Pearson.

McConachie, S., et al. (2006). Task, text, and talk: Literacy for all subjects. *Educational Leadership,* 62 (2), 8-14.

Murphy, P., et al. (2009). Examining the effects of classroom discussion on students' comprehension of text: A meta-analysis. *Journal of Educational Psychology,* 101(3), 740-764.

Pacheco, M.B., David, S.S., & Jiménez, R.T. (2015). Translating pedagogies: Leveraging students' heritage languages in the literacy classroom. *Middle Grades Research Journal,* 10(1), 49.

Pearson, P.D., & Gallagher, M.C. (1983). The instruction of reading comprehension. *Contemporary Education Psychology,* 8, 317-344.

Piaget, J. (1928). *The child's conception of the world.* London: Routledge & Kegan Paul.

Probst, R.E. (2007). Tom Sawyer, teaching, and talking. In K. Beers, R.E. Probst, & L. Rief (Eds.), *Adolescent literacy: Turning promise into practice,* (pp. 43-60). Portsmouth, NH: Heinemann.

Rampey, B.D., Dion, G.S., & Donahue, P.L. (2009). *NAEP 2008 trends in academic progress* (NCES 2009–479). Washington, DC: National Center for Education Statistics, Institute of Education Sciences, & U.S. Department of Education.

Reichenberg, M. (2008). Making students talk about expository texts. *Scandinavian Journal of Educational Research,* 52(1), 17-39.

Schmoker, M. (2006). *Results now: How we can achieve unprecedented improvements in teaching and learning.* Alexandria, VA: ASCD.

Schmoker, M. (2011). *Focus: Elevating the essentials to radically improve student learning.* Alexandria, VA: ASCD.

Seidlitz, J. (2010). *ELPS flip book: A user-friendly guide for academic language instruction.* San Clemente, CA: Canter Press.

Seidlitz, J., & Perryman, B. (2011). *7 steps to a language-rich interactive classroom: Research-based strategies for engaging all students.* San Clemente, CA: Canter Press.

Shanahan T., & Shanahan, C. (2012). What is disciplinary literacy and why does it matter? *Top Language Disorders,* 32 (1), 7-18.

Snow, C. (2010). Academic language and the challenge of reading and learning about science. *Science,* 328, 450-452.

Staarman, J., Krol, K., & van der Meijden, H. (2005). Peer interaction in three collaborative learning environments. *Journal of Classroom Interaction,* 40(1), 29-39.

Tovani, C. (2000). *I read it but I don't get it.* Portland, ME: Stenhouse.

Tovani, C. (2004). *Do I really have to teach reading? Content comprehension, grades 6-12.* Portland, ME: Stenhouse.

Vygotsky, L.S. (1986). *Thought and language.* Cambridge, MA: The MIT Press.

Wertsch, J., del Rio, P., & Alvarez, A. (1995). *Sociocultural studies of mind.* New York, NY: Cambridge University Press.

Williamson, K. (2013). *Transforming literacy learning.* Washington, DC: NCLE Smartbrief.

Zigmond, R. (2008). Ask a provocative question to break the ice. *College Teaching,* 56(3), 154-156.

Zwiers, J. (2008). Building academic language: Essential practices for content classrooms. San Francisco, CA: Jossey-Bass.

Zwiers, J., & Crawford, M. (2011). *Academic conversations: Classroom talk that fosters critical thinking and content understandings.* Portland, ME: Stenhouse.

SEIDLITZ EDUCATION BOOK ORDER FORM

  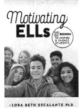   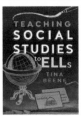

TITLE	PRICE	QTY	TOTAL$	TITLE	PRICE	QTY	TOTAL$
38 Great Academic Language Builders	$24.95			Motivating ELLs: 27 Activities to Inspire & Engage Students	$26.95		
7 Pasos para crear un aula interactiva y rica en lenguaje SPANISH	$29.95			Navigating the ELPS: Using the Standards to Improve Instruction for English Learners	$24.95		
7 Steps to a Language-Rich Interactive Classroom 2ND ED.	$32.95			Navigating the ELPS: Math 2ND ED.	$29.95		
7 Steps To a Language-Rich, Interactive Foreign Language Classroom	$32.95			Navigating the ELPS: Science	$29.95		
				Navigating the ELPS: Social Studies	$29.95		
Boosting Achievement: Reaching Students with Interrupted or Minimal Education	$26.95			Navigating the ELPS: Language Arts and Reading	$34.95		
Content Review & Practice for the TX ESL 154 4TH ED.	$39.95			Optimizando el desarrollo de la lectoescritura SPANISH	$39.95		
Content Review & Practice for the TX Bilingual 164	$39.95			Pathways to Greatness for ELL Newcomers: A Comprehensive Guide for Schools & Teachers	$32.95		
Content Review & Practice for the TX Spanish 190	$39.95			Reading & Writing with English Learners	$29.95		
Diverse Learner Flip Book 2ND ED.	$29.95			RTI for ELLs Fold-Out	$16.95		
DIY PD: A Guide to Self-Directed Learning for Teachers of Multilingual Learners NEW!	$29.95			Sheltered Instruction in Texas: Second Language Acquisition Methods for Teachers of ELs	$29.95		
ELLs in Texas: What Teachers Need to Know 2ND ED.	$34.95			Talk Read Talk Write: A Practical Routine for Learning in All Content Areas K-12 2ND ED.	$32.95		
ELs in Texas: What School Leaders Need to Know 3RD ED.	$34.95			Teaching Social Studies to ELLs	$24.95		
ELPS Flip Book	$19.95			Teaching Science to English Learners	$24.95		
English/Spanish Linguistic and Academic Connections	$29.95			¡Toma la Palabra! SPANISH	$32.95		
Mi Cuaderno de Dictado SPANISH	$7.95			Vocabulary Now! 44 Strategies All Teachers Can Use	$29.95		
	COLUMN 1 TOTAL $				COLUMN 2 TOTAL $		

COLUMN 1+2	$	
DISCOUNT	$	
SHIPPING	$	
TAX	$	
TOTAL	$	

SHIPPING 9% of order total, minimum $14.95
5-7 business days to ship. If needed sooner please call for rates.
TAX EXEMPT? please fax a copy of your certificate along with order.

HOW TO ORDER

PHONE (210) 315-7119 | ONLINE at **www.seidlitzeducation.com**
FAX completed form with payment info to **(949) 200-4384**

NAME

SHIPPING ADDRESS   CITY   STATE, ZIP

PHONE NUMBER   EMAIL ADDRESS

TO ORDER BY FAX
to **(949) 200-4384**
please complete
credit card info *or*
attach purchase order

☐ Visa ☐ MasterCard ☐ Discover ☐ AMEX

CARD #   EXPIRES
          mm/yyyy
SIGNATURE   CVV
          3- or 4- digit code

☐ **Purchase Order attached**
please make
P.O. out to
Seidlitz Education

For information about Seidlitz Education products
and professional development, please contact us at

(210) 315-7119 | kathy@johnseidlitz.com
56 Via Regalo, San Clemente, CA 92673
www.seidlitzeducation.com

Developing
language in every
classroom.™

REV011822

SEIDLITZ PRODUCT ORDER FORM

Three ways to order

- **FAX** completed order form with payment information to **(949) 200-4384**
- **PHONE** order information to **(210) 315-7119**
- **ORDER ONLINE** at **www.seidlitzeducation.com**

Pricing, specifications, and availability subject to change without notice.

TITLE	Price	QTY	TOTAL $
***Instead Of I Don't Know* Poster** For the LOTE Classrom 24" x 36"	**3 pack**			
☐ LOTE FRENCH	$29.85		
☐ LOTE SPANISH	$29.85		
☐ LOTE GERMAN	$29.85		
☐ LOTE ARABIC NEW!	$29.85		
☐ LOTE CHINESE NEW!	$29.85		
		TOTAL $	

TITLE	Price	QTY	TOTAL $
***Instead Of I Don't Know* Poster, 24" x 36"	3 pack**			
☐ Elementary ENGLISH	$29.85		
☐ Secondary ENGLISH	$29.85		
***Instead Of I Don't Know* Posters, 11" x 17"| 20 pack**			
☐ Elementary ENGLISH	$40.00		
☐ Secondary ENGLISH	$40.00		
***Instead Of I Don't Know* Poster, 24" x 36"	3 pack** Elementary SPANISH	$29.85		
***Instead Of I Don't Know* Posters, 11" x 17"	20 pack** Elementary SPANISH	$40.00		
		TOTAL $	

TITLE	Price	QTY	TOTAL $
Academic Language Cards and Activity Booklet, ENGLISH	$19.95		
Academic Language Cards, SPANISH	$9.95		
		TOTAL $	

Please speak in complete sentences.

TITLE	Price	QTY	TOTAL $
Please Speak In Complete Sentences Poster 24" x 36"	**3 pack** ☐ ENGLISH ☐ SPANISH	$29.85		
Please Speak In Complete ***Sentences* Posters, 11" x 17"	20 pack** ☐ ENGLISH ☐ SPANISH	$40.00		
		TOTAL $	

SHIPPING 9% of order total, minimum $14.95
5-7 business days to ship.
If needed sooner please call for rates.

TAX EXEMPT? please fax a copy of your certificate along with order.

GRAND TOTAL	$
DISCOUNT	$
SHIPPING	$
TAX	$
FINAL TOTAL	$

NAME

SHIPPING ADDRESS CITY STATE, ZIP

PHONE NUMBER EMAIL ADDRESS

TO ORDER BY FAX
to **(949) 200-4384**
please complete
credit card info **or**
attach purchase order

☐ Visa ☐ MasterCard ☐ Discover ☐ AMEX

CARD # EXPIRES
 mm/yyyy
SIGNATURE CVV

☐ **Purchase Order**

please make P.O. out to Seidlitz Education